A Charge to Preach

Other Books by the Author

The Minister's Handbook: A Guide for Leadership

Conducting Church Audits: A Guide for Internal Auditors

Preaching that Empowers God's People: Expository Preaching in the 21st Century

A Pastor's Introduction to Church Administration: Administering the 21st Century Church Effectively

A CHARGE TO PREACH
Letters to a Young Preacher

JEREMY W. ODOM

Anointed One Books
Natchitoches

A CHARGE TO PREACH:
LETTERS TO A YOUNG PREACHER

Copyright © 2022 by Jeremy W Odom

All rights reserved.

No part of this book may be reproduced in any form without permission in writing from the publisher, except in the case of brief quotations embodied in critical articles or reviews.

The author has worked to ensure that all information in this book is accurate as of the time of publication. As research and practice advance, however, standards may change. For this reason, it is recommended that readers evaluate the applicability of any recommendations considering particular situations and changing standards.

Anointed One Books has made every effort to trace the ownership of all quotes. In the event of a question arising from the use of a quote, we regret any error made and will be pleased to make the necessary correction in future printings and editions of this book.

ISBN 978-0-9970-9566-1

Library of Congress Control Number: 2022917707

All Scripture quotations, unless otherwise indicated, are taken from the *New King James Version®*. Copyright © 1982 by Thomas Nelson. Used by permission. All rights reserved.

Scripture designated KJV is taken from the *King James Version®* of the Bible.

Printed in the United States of America

Dedicated with love and respect
To my beloved Pastor and cousin,
Rev. Frank Douglas Randle, Jr.
And to all who stand to share
In the burdens and benefits of
preaching God's Gospel

But I keep under my body, and bring it into subjection: lest that by any means, when I have preached to others, I myself should be a castaway.

I Corinthians 9:27 KJV

Contents

i. Acknowledgements .... *i*
ii. Foreword .... *iii*
iii. *Dear Young Preacher* Introduction Letter .... *v*

1. The Preacher & His Calling 1
2. The Mind of the Preacher 9
3. The Preacher & His Health 19
4. The Preacher & His Preaching 25
5. The Preacher & His Demons 35
6. Practical Instructions for the Young Preacher 47
7. To Pastor or Not to Pastor…That is the Question 55
8. The Preacher & His Gifts 63
A. Grace-Gifts Inventory 77
B. Poem: *A Preacher's Prayer* 89
C. Selected Bibliography 91

A Charge to Preach: *Letters to A Young Preacher*

Acknowledgements

To God be Praise! I am truly indebted to so many who have coached, mentored, taught, and prayed for me all these years in ministry. I recognize and acknowledge that I could not be who I am without the contributory seeds that each of these individuals have planted in my life. First, and foremost, I acknowledge my one true boss – Jesus Christ who found this broken vessel fit for service in His Ministry.

Next, I want to acknowledge those sages who took time with me to teach me how to carry and conduct myself as God's preacher. My late pastors: Dr. Joseph D. Dupree and Rev. William Batts who encouraged and demanded my education and training. I also remember former seminary instructors: the late Rev. Tony Wallace, the late Rev. John A. Robinson, the late Rev. G. Stanley Lewis, Dr. Herbert V. Baptiste, Sr., and Mr. Paul Morgan, Sr.

Respectfully, I acknowledge some from the community who played undeniable roles in my Christian development: the late Mrs. Daisy Jones, Rev. James Graham, Ms. Mildred Dean Joseph, the late Mr. Ben D. Johnson, Sr., the late Rev. Thomas Small, the late David and Delores Moore and LTC (R) Christopher Sylvia.

I have also been fortunate to have many role models in the Ministry to offer guidance and encouragement for which I am certainly grateful: the late Dr. B. J. Maxon, the late Dr. Mallery Callahan, Sr., the late Dr. Solomon Shorter, Sr., Dr. Mitchell Herndon, Sr., Rev. Frank D. Randle, Jr., Dr. Joe S. Green, President S. C. Dixon, Rev. Michael Otkins, Sr., Dr. Larry Cross, Dr. Cornelius Tilman, Dr. Willie Gable, Sr., Dr. Bobby Showers, Sr. and Dr. Joseph Martin, Sr.

I thank my parents – Early Odom, Jr. and Carolyn Essex – as well as other family members who will never be forgotten for their

Acknowledgements

contributions: my late Aunt Evelyn Davis Caldwell, my aunts Wanda, Claudia and Toni, and my brother Greg.

A great debt of gratitude is due to the Louisiana Ministerial Association, Inc. and its current president Rev. Mekell V. Toussaint as well as my home church Damascus Missionary Baptist Church for your prayers and support.

I also commend my church family at Mount Harmon Baptist Church for welcoming me as a part of the family. Your support and encouragement have not gone unnoticed, and I am most appreciative to have you all in my life.

Finally, I thank God for my first pastoral assignment – Bright Morning Star Missionary Baptist Church – whose members taught me how to Pastor and I am forever indebted to them and will always hold a solemn space for you in my heart.

Foreword

Reverend Odom has compiled a practical guide for the young preacher seeking to begin a life of sanctified service to the Lord and His church. Written by a man who has served the church in many capacities, including, Pastor, Associate Minister and staff member, he shares important lessons learned and pitfalls to be avoided.

Replete with valuable scriptures and wisdom from sages across the centuries, *A Charge to Preach – Letters to A Young Preacher* will be an invaluable reference even for the preacher who has been "on the wall" for a season.

Dr. Cornelius Tilton has been Senior Pastor of the Irish Channel Christian Fellowship in New Orleans for over 35 years and President of Christian Bible College of Louisiana training future Pastors and Christian leaders for almost 25 years.

A Charge to Preach: *Letters to A Young Preacher*

Dear Young Preacher

Congratulations on being called to the Ministry of our Lord and Savior Jesus Christ! It is a great undertaking that you should not take lightly or for granted. As a minister, you have been called to do a great work as a servant and ambassador of Christ. But what all does it entail? When will I get my own church?

Before I go any further, I find it necessary to clarify that "young preacher" has to do with ministry experience and not age. One of the most common challenges among young ministers is knowing where they fit in. If you get nothing else from the pages that follow, find you a seasoned pastor to sit under for at least three years.

I would recommend that it is one who has at least ten more years of preaching experience than yourself. Your pastor must be able to correct you in love and hold your respect as your pastor. A preacher without a pastor is worthless to the cause. The early years of your ministry should be focused on learning your craft. In this day and time, it is prudent to go to seminary and learn the proper way to prepare and deliver a sermon.

You will find embodied in this little book some helpful information that I have learned from attending various conventions and conferences over the last 20+ years that are vital instruction for young preachers. I invite pastors to share these and other pearls of wisdom with their associate ministers.

At the close of each chapter, you will be asked a series of questions for personal reflection. These questions and your responses will call for you to make an honest assessment of yourself. There are also a few more points that you are suggested to discuss with you pastor. Remember, the relationship between you and your pastor is vitally important as he is ultimately responsible for grooming you in your ministry. Have an open mind and be ready to gleam from his years of experience when you talk with him.

I plead with you brother that you will stir up the gift of God that is in you. Let the materials presented herein be a blessing aid to your ministry. It will behoove you to always remember that many are called but only a few chosen.

Kingdom Building,

Dr. Jeremy W. Odom

Chapter One

THE PREACHER

HIS CALLING

Traditionally, the Baptist Church has encouraged, equipped, and employed the service of persons called by God to preach the Gospel of our Lord and Savior Jesus Christ. By recognizing a calling to the ministry, one should publicly declare such during the invitational period of the church service which allows the Pastor and Church to acknowledge and bless the new minister's calling.

Preaching the Bible is a unique enterprise in that it cannot be done effectively when something is off in the personal life of the preacher. God desires His vessel to be clean all the way to the preacher's heart. Know this that it is impossible to preach the Word of God effectively while failing to meet personal financial obligations or living in sin.

> *Dear Young Preacher,*
>
> *Your personal life and discipline can make or break your preaching ministry. People will outright reject what you say if it does not match what you do (how you live).*

Chapter One • *The Preacher & His Calling*

Paul admonished Timothy to take notice of his character and integrity as well as his teaching in I Timothy 4:16. First Timothy 3:1-7 and Titus 1:5-9 provide a heart checkup for the preacher. First Thessalonians 2:1-12 is possibly the most intimate and intensely personal passage in that Paul sets forth his own convictions about the benchmarks of the ministry characterized by character and integrity.

- God-given mission. Today's image of the effective preacher is of an unusually handsome man with the voice of an actor and mind of a scholar. However, according to Paul, there must exist a strong sense of mission. It is the commitment to the Gospel that made him bold under the most difficult of trials. Understand that the work of preaching is no easy task. When you set out to serve the Lord, you can bank on the fact though you will experience obstacles along the way that your sense of mission will keep you from being overcome.

- Genuine motivation. False teachers were often nomadic during Paul's time. Unfortunately, we face this same problem today. Charlatans utilize television, YouTube, social media, and radio causing many to be skeptical of preachers in general. Consequently, the motives of the preacher must be right. Too much flattery is present in modern preaching. The preacher should never flatter those to whom he preaches for personal gain or praise. We must constantly ask ourselves *Is my preaching genuinely motivated.*

- Gentle manner. The preacher should follow Paul's example. Paul had a compassionate and loving heart. Real preaching is not only the delivery of a sermon, but the outflow of life as well. There is no 40-hour work week. The preacher must be available to sow into the lives of the people any time. The preacher must also be firm and truthful as well recognizing his sacred responsibility to teach people how to live a Christian life.

Dr. William E. Flippin, Sr. points out in his book, *God's Order: Order in the Church and Pulpit*, that everyone involved in the confession or announcement of a calling should strictly adhere to a specific set of guidelines. The candidate initiates the process by making an appointment with the Pastor to acknowledge the call to the ministry. After receiving the counsel of the Pastor, the candidate makes a public confession of said calling before the congregation. It is important to note that until the initial sermon is delivered in the candidate's home church, the candidate is still considered a lay member and should not be sitting or doing assignments from the pulpit. After the candidate has made adequate study, prayer and preparation, the Pastor should schedule the first sermon. A License to preach the Gospel is presented to the candidate from his church following the first sermon.

Many young preachers are set up for failure when there is no foundation of prayer and preparation. It is of utmost importance that the young preacher enters a period of training and further preparation under his Pastor's instruction.

> *Dear Young Preacher,*
>
> *Make no never mind about it, the bulk if not all your preaching instruction will originate with your Pastor. I am convinced that EVERY Pastor has something of immense value to offer the young preachers who serve under them.*

Chapter One • *The Preacher & His Calling*

Just as a person's driver's license can be revoked for refusing to obey the rules of the road, it is important for young preachers to understand that the church or Pastor may revoke the License to Preach in the case of conduct unbecoming a minister. Take notice young preacher that the Pastor will determine a date for ordination only after an appropriate time of oversight. He is the one who maintains the responsibility for evaluating your commitment and service to the Lord, the Word, the church, and the work of the local congregation. During this time, you should be focusing on getting to know his theology of ministry and personal vision for the church.

While the License authorizes you to preach, there are some things that you cannot do in the Baptist church prior to becoming ordained (i.e., pastor a church, baptize, administer the Lord's supper, perform marriages, or bury the dead). You may still visit with and pray for the sick and shut in. Before we talk about ordination, it is prudent for us to revisit the role of the Associate Minister.

> *Dear Young Preacher,*
>
> *Your role as an Associate Minister is primarily to support the Pastor actively and cheerfully in his effort to spiritually nurture the congregation. This can only be accomplished through steadfast commitment and loyalty to the kingdom of God.*

The English word "ordain" has three different meanings: (1) to set in order, (2) to establish, and (3) to set apart for a special function. In common ecclesiastical usage, ordination commonly refers to special status accorded to ministers through officially sanctioned rites. Flippin writes that a young preacher desiring to be considered for ordination should meet one or more of the following criteria:

- Receive the call to pastor an existing church
- Receive the call to serve on the ministerial staff of an existing congregation
- Receive the call to start a new church or mission. It is important for the young preacher to understanding that this is not a personal call but generally originates from an organized ecclesiastical council or board.
- Receive the call to the mission field, either domestic or international.
- Complete an approved course of study taught by the pastor after he has determined your readiness.
- Graduate from an accredited Bible college or seminary.

While most branches of the Christian church ordain individuals who have received a public and formal call into the Gospel ministry, the requirements for ordination differ from church to church. Churches historically agree on three major prerequisites in the ordination candidate's life:
1. Evidence of salvation
2. Evidence of a divine call or vocation
3. Formal call from a recognized New Testament ministry

Candidates for ordination should demonstrate sincere conviction and knowledge of their respective denomination's doctrine, especially in areas relevant to the specific ministry of calling. Although preachers are normally ordained in their own congregation, there are exceptions where the pastor and congregation agree and recognize the need for ordination.

Over time, new models of pastoral ministry as team ministry and associate pastors emerged due to expanded needs and ministry requirements. Proper preparation of the preacher is probably more

Chapter One • *The Preacher & His Calling*

essential now than in previous years with the exploration of new ministry concepts and models. For this reason, churches continue to carefully consider candidates for ordination. Any preacher that offers himself as a candidate for ordination should have no objection to participating in a formal training process. Remember Young Preacher that your call to minister also includes the call to prepare. Training is a requirement, not an option!

If the minister does not possess the means to attend seminary or a major training academy, there are other options to consider. Church-operated Bible schools and institutes are just a couple of options that present the minister with opportunities for training in the religious community. No matter the path chosen, it is this writer's belief that some form of professional training should be required of every ordination candidate.

Preacher candidates are required to write a statement of belief or spiritual autobiography outlining their personal fundamentals of faith in some churches. This is a helpful tool for the candidate who desires to organize his thoughts. It also provides members of the ordination council the opportunity to prepare relevant questions for the formal evaluation of the candidate.

The candidate's personal character, ethics, and morals constitute areas of crucial concern. The ministry of the kingdom must remain a proving ground for righteousness. The importance of strong moral fiber for preachers cannot be stressed enough. Ministry is a dual call into service. We serve God primarily, and serving God demands that we serve the people of God. The preacher must be of impeccable integrity knowing that failing to live by the standard he preaches from the pulpit causes him to forfeit the respect of the flock thereby bringing shame upon the household of faith.

Ministry is an undertaking of eternal importance, and we must rigorously screen those who present themselves as candidates for this work. If Lawyers are required to pass the bar exam to practice law and Physicians a medical exam, should not there be an examination and assessment of the abilities of they who would carry the Gospel. Appropriate qualifying trials and examinations are an affirmation of the solemn responsibility of Christian ministry.

> *Dear Young Preacher,*
>
> *God's calling alone is adequate grounds for ministry and no one may add anything to God's call!*

Your calling from God is intensely personal, but understand the church maintains the right to validate and confirm that calling through ordination. To this end, you must be prepared to explain and clearly articulate this inward experience through outward conversation with church leaders. Therefore, careful thought and reasoned preparation can help you defend your calling to others who must discern your readiness for ordination.

As a minister at your home church, your first responsibility is to be an integral part of the worship experience there. As such, whenever you are not preaching at another church, a mission, or prison, you should be present at worship. This includes the weekly Bible study period and Sunday School. As a young preacher, you should never resent pastoral guidance, but diligently seek opportunities to learn from your pastor's experience. When you have devoted yourself to the study of God's word, it should be a rewarding experience for you to serve as a Sunday School, Bible School or even Vacation Bible School teacher.

Chapter One • *The Preacher & His Calling*

Personal Reflection

- How does my character and integrity relate to that of Paul?

- Am I sure of my personal salvation?

- Have I really been called to preach?

- How have I made proof of my ministry?

Discuss with your Pastor

- What ministry am I feeling led into? Why?

- Discuss the expectations you hold of your Pastor.

- Discuss your Pastor's vision and how you can support it.

Chapter Two

THE MIND

of

THE PREACHER

Those who are familiar with the United Negro College Fund are aware that a mind is a terrible thing to waste. The sentiments of this statement are especially appropriate for the young preacher, for truly, the worst thing a young preacher can do is to waste their mind! It is of utmost importance that the young preacher thinks right, wills right, perceives right and reasons right! Ralph Waldo Emerson said, "A man is what he thinks about all day long."

For as he thinks in his heart, so is he. [Proverbs 23:7a NKJV]

Make no mistake about it, Young Preacher, while you can fool everybody else with your clothes, charm, cologne, good looks, preaching, prancing, and singing, God knows your mind and your thoughts!

And Jesus knowing their thoughts said, wherefore think ye evil in your hearts? [Matthew 9:4 KJV]

The LORD knoweth the thoughts of man, that they are vanity. [Psalm 94:11 KJV]

Chapter Two • *The Mind of the Preacher*

O LORD, thou hast searched me, and known me. Thou knowest my downsitting and mine uprising, thou understandest my thought afar off. [Psalm 139:1-2 KJV]

John R. W. Stott says that the preacher should never be an example of "the misery and menace of mindless Christianity." God, through His Word, will expose what is really on your mind!

For the word of God is quick, and powerful, and sharper than any twoedged sword, piercing even to the dividing asunder of soul and spirit, and of the joints and marrow, and is a discerner of the thoughts and intents of the heart. [Hebrews 4:12 KJV]

> *Dear Young Preacher,*
>
> *YOU have been created to think; created to use your mind!*

So God created man in his own image, in the image of God created he him; male and female created he them. [Genesis 1:27 KJV]

Come now, and let us reason together, saith the LORD: though your sins be as scarlet, they shall be as white as snow; though they be red like crimson, they shall be as wool. [Isaiah 1:18 KJV]

For my thoughts are not your thoughts, neither are your ways my ways, saith the LORD. For as the heavens are higher than the earth, so are my ways higher than your ways, and my thoughts than your thoughts. [Isaiah 55:8-9 KJV]

It is impossible to understand God's Word unless you utilize your mind to comprehend God's Word. For God's Word itself would be meaningless unless Man has the capacity, the mind, to grasp God's Word!

A Charge to Preach: *Letters to A Young Preacher*

Jesus answered and said unto them, Ye do err, not knowing the scriptures, nor the power of God. [Matthew 22:29 KJV]

It would behoove the young preacher to hone his skill of persuasion knowing that it is virtually impossible for a Preacher to win the lost without being persuasive. It is also virtually impossible for a Preacher to be persuasive without using his mind!

Knowing therefore the terror of the Lord, we persuade men; but we are made manifest unto God; and I trust also are made manifest in your consciences. [II Corinthians 5:11 KJV]

Now when they had passed through Amphipolis and Apollonia, they came to Thessalonica, where was a synagogue of the Jews: And Paul, as his manner was, went in unto them, and three sabbath days reasoned with them out of the scriptures, Opening and alleging, that Christ must needs have suffered, and risen again from the dead; and that this Jesus, whom I preach unto you, is Christ. And some of them believed, and consorted with Paul and Silas; and of the devout Greeks a great multitude, and of the chief women not a few. [Acts 17:1-4 KJV]

The preacher's mind should always be properly focused so that good and Holy thoughts prevail rather than Evil ones.

We have thought of thy lovingkindness, O God, in the midst of thy temple. [Psalm 48:9 KJV]

The thoughts of the righteous are right: but the counsels of the wicked are deceit. [Proverbs 12:5 KJV]

Finally, brethren, whatsoever things are true, whatsoever things are honest, whatsoever things are just, whatsoever things are pure, whatsoever things are lovely, whatsoever things are of good report; if there be any virtue, and if there be any praise, think on these things. [Philippians 4:8 KJV]

Chapter Two • *The Mind of the Preacher*

And be not conformed to this world: but be ye transformed by the renewing of your mind, that ye may prove what is that good, and acceptable, and perfect, will of God. For I say, through the grace given unto me, to every man that is among you, not to think of himself more highly than he ought to think; but to think soberly, according as God hath dealt to every man the measure of faith. [Romans 12: 2-3 KJV]

The thoughts of the wicked are an abomination to the LORD: but the words of the pure are pleasant words. [Proverbs 15:26 KJV]

O Jerusalem, wash thine heart from wickedness, that thou mayest be saved. How long shall thy vain thoughts lodge within thee. [Jeremiah 4:14 KJV]

For out of the heart proceed evil thoughts, murders, adulteries, fornications, thefts, false witnesses, blasphemies: [Matthew 15:19 KJV]

>   *Dear Young Preacher,*
>
>   *Did you know that there are five things that can prove to be enemies to the mind of the preacher?*

1. Television softens and seduces the mind to only think about things that are trivial, trite, and notoriously immoral. How can a Preacher strengthen his mind while constantly watching **One Life to Live, Days of Our Lives, As the World Turns, Wheel of Fortune, P Valley** and **The Haves and the Have Nots**?

2. Secular music, as well as much of Contemporary Gospel Music over-emphasizes emotion, sex, and sensuality, and de-

emphasizes thought, meditation and serious reflection, when it come to the words and the Word!

3. Constant socializing, convention attending, conferencing, and partying are activities that steal precious quality time from the Preacher and kidnap the Preacher from quiet serene places where he can study and concentrate.

Be still, and know that I am God: I will be exalted among the heathen, I will be exalted in the earth. [Psalm 46:10 KJV]

And in the morning, rising up a great while before day, he went out, and departed into a solitary place, and there prayed. [Mark 1:35 KJV]

4. Written sermons, sermons on tapes and CDs, and YouTube sermons that are watched, read, or listened to for the primary purpose of preaching another preacher's message are true diabolical enemies of the preacher's mind. Stealing and copying another Preacher's style and message will sadly stunt, retard, and delay a young Preacher's mental, intellectual and spiritual growth! For Young Preacher, E.V. Hill is great, Caesar Clark is great, C. L. Franklin is great, F. D. Sampson, Sr. is great, but when are YOU going to be the Preacher God called YOU to be?

5. A heavy emotional involvement with the wrong sister is an Enemy! The wrong sister will satanically possess, cloud, and strain a Preacher's mind so, until they will only be able to think about that sister instead of thinking about the things of God.

Set your affection on things above, not on things on earth. [Colossians 3:2 KJV]

Chapter Two • *The Mind of the Preacher*

A double minded man is unstable in all his ways. [James 1:8 KJV]

Dear Young Preacher,

Be encouraged that there are also at least four great allies to the mind of the preacher.

1. Diligent study of the Scriptures conditions, disciplines and focuses the mind to think Biblically, redemptively, and Christianly! For nothing is sadder than a Preacher who thinks like the world. The only way for the Preacher to acquire and exemplify the Mind of the Lord is for the Preacher to study and know the Word of the Lord! It has been said that the Preacher is to think God's thoughts after Him.

   Thou wilt keep him in perfect peace, whose mind is stayed on thee: because he trusteth in thee. [Isaiah 26:3 KJV]

   Let this mind be in you, which was also in Christ Jesus: [Philippians 2:5 KJV]

   For who hath known the mind of the Lord, that he may instruct him? But we have the mind of Christ. [I Corinthians 2:16 KJV]

   Jesus said unto him, Thou shalt love the Lord thy God with all thy heart, and with all thy soul, and with all thy mind. [Matthew 22:37 KJV]

2. Reading insightful spiritual books by reputable authors is a valuable ally. Good books speak to Biblical truths that can be identified in and applied to everyday living! While I do not

mean to challenge the theology of indie authors, I feel the need to caution the young preacher to give more credence to the author of the work as opposed to the name of the book. We live in a time when any and everybody can publish anything if they have the money.

3. Listening critically to great and thoughtful preaching challenges the young Preacher's mind to take the Biblical text seriously. This Gospel that we carry is too valuable, too precious, and too expedient to be made a mockery of. It is a sad preacher who never wants to hear another preacher. Listening attentively to other preachers will also challenge the young preacher to creatively search for points in the text. More importantly, it should encourage the young preacher to grasp the utmost importance of preparation and study.

4. Quietness and solitude provide an atmosphere where deep and clear thinking can emerge and surface. Henri J. M. Nouwen says, "Silence makes us pilgrims." The Preacher needs to become a pilgrim – a spiritual traveler – if he is to discover the hidden and rich gems of Truth!

Many young preachers play all sorts of "mind games" with themselves and each other due to their insecurity, inexperience, and lack of direction. Consider these next five statements as warning signs that the young preacher is playing "mind games."

1. "I don't need to go to school, the Holy Spirit will be my teacher." (II Timothy 2:15)

2. "Because my church is bigger than his, I am far more important than he is." (Romans 12:2; Genesis 1:27)

Chapter Two • *The Mind of the Preacher*

3. "The reason why I don't like them or like to be around them is because their popularity has gone to their head." (I Samuel 18:6-11)

4. "If I just dress like a Preacher, look like a Preacher, walk like a Preacher, kick my leg out when I'm standing behind the pulpit like a Preacher, wave my hand and stand up like a Preacher, then I must be a Preacher." (Matthew 23:27; I Samuel 16:7)

5. "I can drink as much as I want to; I can smoke as much dope as I want to; I can have as many women as I want to; I can have homosexual affairs if I want to; I can lie, steal, cheat and gamble as much as I want to, and still have Power when I Preach." (I Peter 1:16; Leviticus 19:2)

Personal Reflection

- What are some ways that I can hone my skills of persuasion?

- Have I polluted my mind with anything that can negatively affect my ministry?

- Am I developing my own style or mimicking someone else's preaching style?

- What tools am I currently developing to strengthen my mind for ministry?

Discuss with your Pastor

- Discuss your personal struggles guarding your mind and what steps can be taken to safeguard your ministry.

- Discuss some reputable authors that you can read.

Chapter Three

THE PREACHER

HIS HEALTH

> *Dear Young Preacher,*
>
> *God wants you to be healthy! Great care must be taken by the preacher to maintain an overall healthy lifestyle. This includes your spiritual, mental, and physical health together. How effective your ministry will be depending on the dedication you have to taking care of yourself.*

The preacher must not only spend time preparing the message, but he must also prepare himself. God's Word is not preached apart from human instrumentality. It is prudent for the preacher to build certain qualities on the foundation of God's call, the Word, worship, and anointing. His consideration of several aspects of self-preparation makes this possible. Not only should the preacher give attention to his character and integrity, but he must not neglect his physical fitness.

There exists currently in America, a great push for healthy living. Hardly anywhere you go will you not find people jogging trying to

Chapter Three • The Preacher & His Health

get in shape. People are becoming more aware of the eating habits, counting calories, and pushing back from the table. This interest in good health is considered to have a strong biblical foundation.

According to the Bible, the believer's body is a sacred temple of the Holy Spirit, and the believer understands the obligation of maintaining said temple in good shape. The preacher is better equipped to serve the Lord when he takes care of his body. Consequently, preachers must concern themselves with physical fitness. There exist several essentials for this task – intentionality, exercise, healthy eating, and plenty of rest.

INTENTIONALITY

Physical fitness is an often-neglected area for many preachers. The preacher is so engulfed in the Lord's work and the myriad of church activities that he often fails to take adequate time tending to the needs of his body. According to Jerry Vines (author of *Power in the Pulpit*), the preacher's message loses credibility due to the poor condition of the vessel being used to deliver it. Some preachers minimize the importance of physical fitness claiming it an improper waste of time to engage in various forms of recreation. Dear Young Preacher, it is okay to take the necessary time to keep your body in good condition.

Be warned that failing to find time to maintain physical fitness forces the preacher to find time for physical illness. It has been said that the body and soul live so close together they catch one another's diseases. It is impossible to benefit one part of your life without benefiting the whole. It is God's intention for his servants to have sound minds and bodies. Seeing that the body is the vehicle God uses to communicate His Word to men, the preacher must keep it in good condition.

EXERCISE

The preacher should schedule blocks of time for physical exercise. The countless hours he devotes to study and sermon preparation are indeed a most tiring form of the preacher's work. It may not be as easy for the preacher to bounce back immediately from this intensive mental labor as it is for one to recover after strenuous physical activity.

The lack of regular exercise is a leading cause of lethargy. By failing to exercise the physical body, the preacher will come to experience his body tiring easily and lacking energy. Physical exercise builds stamina and improves the cardiovascular system. The preacher may opt to jog or swim for half-an-hour three days a week to get started. Shooting hoops can prove rewarding as well as it not only gives the benefit of a strenuous workout but also provides the preacher with a ministry opportunity. At the end of the day, it doesn't matter so much the form of exercise just if you do something. The preacher is cautioned to have a complete physical from his doctor PRIOR to beginning a new exercise regime.

It is important to remember that time spent exercising is never wasted. The preacher will find himself more productive during working hours because of the time he takes each week exercising. He will soon discover his ability to think more clearly as well as his powers of creativity heightened.

HEALTHY EATING

Developing good eating habits helps the preacher's physical well-being. Not only should the preacher eat healthy, but he also needs to keep his weight under control. A well-balanced diet helps to accomplish this. Eat only when you are hungry and avoid snacking in between meals. Dear Young Preacher, please do not fall prey to gluttony after you preach. Normally, tensions are being released immediately after preaching thus causing greater hunger and thirst than usual. These factors unfortunately can lead to overindulgence.

Eating large portions at late hours also contribute to poor sleep and obesity. The preacher should keep bread and sweets to a minimum. By cutting down on sugar intake, the preacher protects his preaching voice as sugar and milk tend to form mucus. Eat plenty of green, leafy vegetables and be sure you have an adequate intake of bulk.

> Dear Young Preacher,
>
> There is no need to become a health-food enthusiast. Just consider proper eating habits. You will find these habits to be good for your physical well-being as well as their effects to be a positive testimony. Think about it. How can we tell others Christ can give them power over drugs and alcohol when we seem unable to control our eating habits?

Several Christ-centered dietary programs have been developed in recent years which have helped many people get a handle on healthy eating. They even have different areas of concentration. No matter the approach you take, be aware that resources are available to help develop healthy eating habits.

REST

It is an understatement that most preachers do not get enough rest. Many appear to be night owls and seem to come alive in the late hours. Obviously, this practice makes it harder to get up early in the morning. The preacher should make a conscious effort to go to bed earlier knowing that will pay off the following day. Sleep experts say that each hour of sleep before midnight is worth two hours of sleep after midnight. This theory has proven true for most people.

The preacher especially needs adequate rest the night before preaching. Try taking the day prior completely off. Relax your mind completely and do some things that you enjoy doing. Spend some leisurely time with your wife and children. Don't think too much about your sermon the next day. Prior to going to bed, get alone for a *brief* time to go over your morning message attempting to saturate your soul with the content of the sermon. Spend some time in prayer, talking to the Lord about the message. Then go to bed for a good night's rest and when the morning comes, you will be rested and ready.

Personal Reflection

- How is my overall health? Am I neglecting myself?

- How can I increase my physical fitness?

- How am I sleeping?

Discuss with your Pastor

- Discuss ways to promote healthy living in your ministry.

Chapter Four

THE PREACHER

HIS PREACHING

According to A. W. Tozer, too many Christians wish to enjoy the thrill of feeling right without having to endure the inconvenience of being right. Recent years has produced many celebrities in the church but not nearly enough servants. Warren Wiersbe writes in *The Integrity Crisis that Every Associate Minister Needs to Ponder* that we must accept the bad news about ourselves before we can believe the good news about Jesus. It is what we believe that determines how we behave and what we become.

The careful study of how sermons are to be developed and preached is known as homiletics. Outstanding preachers have outstanding homiletics. Poor preachers have poor homiletics. Homiletics is the art and science and preaching.

But hath in due times manifested his word through preaching, which is committed unto me according to the commandment of God our Saviour; (Titus 1:3 KJV)

Preaching is communicating divine truth to your people. It is the most important calling on earth. Even more important than being King (Queen) of England or President of the United States. As

Chapter Four • The Preacher & His Preaching

such, it is imperative for the preacher to remember to preach by God's power rather than man's wisdom (c.f. I Corinthians 2:4-5). Preach using laymen's terms as opposed to enticing words.

Hermeneutics is the science and methodology of applying certain principles for the interpretation of Scripture.

Exegesis is the proper "pulling out" of truths and insights from the Scripture or a given text. It is impossible to have a proper exegesis without diligent study coupled with the aid of the Holy Ghost. In contrast, eisegesis occurs when a preacher interjects his own opinions and viewpoints into the scripture. This action results in an incorrect understanding of the text.

> *Dear Young Preacher,*
>
> *Remember the lack of serious study and consecration will always yield an incorrect eisegesis instead of the correct exegesis.*

There are four basic types of preaching available to the preacher.
1. Topical Preaching is when you preach from a topic, and your points come from the topic itself, with little reference to the biblical text per se.
2. Textual Preaching is when you preach from a particular text, and all your points come from that text.
3. Expository Preaching is when you preach from an extended portion of Scripture, whereby your points therein are analyzed meticulously (i.e., context, grammar, word study, syntax, tense, etc.)
4. Narrative Preaching is when you retell a biblical story based upon a given text, providing insights and commentary along the way or after.

Many believe that expository preaching is the best discipline for the young preacher just starting out, but he must take note that

Jesus Himself exercised the narrative style of preaching (c.f. Matthew 13:34).

When preparing the sermon, the preacher must ensure he is on good terms with the Holy Spirit so that he can clearly hear Him (c.f. John 10:3-4). It is the Holy Spirit that will assist the preacher remain focused and undistracted by other spirits (political correctness, personal prejudices, unresolved emotions and/or fears, etc.). The Holy Spirit will literally guide the preacher into the truths and depths of Scripture (c.f. John 16:13).

> *Dear Young Preacher,*
>
> *When you are on good terms with the Holy Spirit, you will have anointed power in the pulpit that will be unmistakable (c.f. Acts 1:8).*

The preacher needs to thoroughly know his Bible, particularly the chapter AND book of his chosen text (c.f. Matthew 22:29). He should be consecrated through prayer all throughout the sermon process – from conception to delivery. The preacher should develop a thesis sentence. This sentence explains what the preacher wants to get his audience to see and understand in his sermon.

Preachers – especially young preachers – should carefully study the sermons and preaching techniques of great preachers (past and present) and try to hear great preachers as often as possible.

David therefore himself calleth him Lord; and whence is he then his son? And the common people heard him gladly. (Mark 12:37 KJV)

As soon as possible young preacher, develop a homiletical mind. Train your mind to detect sermon ideas in things that you read, observe, experience, and/or hear.

Chapter Four • The Preacher & His Preaching

And why take ye thought for raiment? Consider the lilies of the field, how they grow; they toil not, neither do they spin: And yet I say unto you, That even Solomon in all his glory was not arrayed like one of these. Wherefore, if God so clothe the grass of the field, which to day is, and to morrow is cast into the oven, shall he not much more clothe you, O ye of little faith? (Matthew 6:28-30 KJV)

Be intentional about building up a good reference section in your personal library that should include at a minimum: a good Dictionary, a good Dictionary of Biblical Words, good commentaries on books of the Bible, and a volume categorizing the words of Jesus by subject.

> *Dear Young Preacher,*
>
> *It is important to understand the gravity of assignment you accept as a spokesman for the Almighty. You must take care to ensure that you have made adequate preparation prior to the presentation of your sermon.*

These guiding principles are mere observations from my twenty plus years of ministry.

1. Avoid prefacing any scripture reading with *you've probably heard this before* or the like. The preacher should read the scriptures boldly and without excuse. The scripture is important enough to read confidently – after all, you found it important enough to include. The congregation doesn't need the preacher giving a reason to tune out what he is saying.

2. Avoid telling stories and then haphazardly tossing in a scripture or two to make it seem like a sermon. Your scriptures should be the basis of your message. Your illustrations must hold for a purpose making the scriptures and spiritual lessons come to life.

3. Sometimes it is okay to resist the urge to lead out in a congregational hymn before preaching. Just because you can preach does not necessarily mean you can sing.

4. Remember the arm's length rule when preaching. If you find yourself more than an arm's length from the lectern, you are out of bounds. Don't say another word until you have returned to the proper preaching zone.

5. The preacher would be wise to properly utilize metaphors and analogies when preaching. The gift of preaching requires the use of both feelings and logic. By engaging both sides of the human brain, true learning occurs.

6. Your primary responsibility is to teach from God's word. The preferred task of changing the culture to conform to God may be difficult but is rewarding. Never be afraid to teach.

7. Avoid spending time saying how unsure you were of what you wanted to talk about. Your introduction should focus on what is you came to say.

8. Remember that you are preaching to an entire congregation as opposed to an individual. Turning and facing someone to speak directly to them while preaching is bad manners. Always bear in mind that preaching is a congregational moment in worship. Avoid turning your back on the congregation.

9. Never, ever, EVER say *I really didn't want to be here today.* The preacher must understand that he is on God's errand. It is never okay to excuse yourself from giving your very best in service. Always maintain the presumption of the audience that what you have to say is worthwhile, important, and beneficial to them.

10. Focus your sermon. Again, it is necessary to know your thesis statement.

11. Please do not beg for a response. If your call necessitates you begging for a response, you may want to hang up that message and try dialing again using exegetical and expositional assistance next time. The people know when they feel the urge to share an amen.

12. Know your audience if possible. Tailor the message for those who are in the audience. Understanding the spiritual, social and/or emotional needs of the listeners will increase the effectiveness of the preacher's sermon.

13. If the preacher is going to preach by the Spirit, he must prepare for the assignment long before the delivery. The preacher will not be effective in this approach if he fails to spend uninterrupted time with the Spirit.

14. Never attempt the use of subliminal messaging in your prayers. Your prayers should be directed to God alone, not seeking a response from those who hear it. If you have a message for the people, give it directly to the people. Prayer without real intent profits nothing but keeping God's commandments invites God's spirit to reside in power within us.

15. Prayer and fasting before being asked to speak is just as important as praying and fasting when preparing to speak. The best time to start preparing for a sermon is before being asked. Maintain a daily spiritual frame of mind so that the burning question is not *what I am going to preach* but rather *how do I condense everything the Lord has shown me!*

16. Understand that every scripture you study during preparation does not have to be included in your sermon. In preparation, some information will only be useful for the preacher's growth and development – though on topic, it may be viewed as information overload in delivery to the congregation.

17. The preacher's sermon should always call for action and response from listeners. Good sermons offer a purpose and call the sinner to action. The sermon need not only call for change but should offer steps to change.

18. Take care not to overemphasize your inadequacies as a Minister from the pulpit. Deal with any broken relationships prior to entering the pulpit. Many preachers are their own worst enemy in that they spend a lot of time expounding on their own shortcomings during the sermon rather than ministering to the needs of the people.

19. Remember that preaching can never be about the preacher. All glory belongs to God, so the preacher does well to remember John's prayer (John 3:31).

20. Look to the Holy Spirit for your true reward. The preacher begins diminishing his preaching ability when he begins desiring the praise of the people rather than strength from God.

21. Remember you cannot preach it all at one setting. The mark of a good speech delivery involves developing an attention-grabbing introduction, a dynamic conclusion, and keeping the two as close together as possible.

22. Commit the scriptures in your sermon to memory. The preacher should develop the ability to read a scripture while maintaining eye contact to the congregation.

23. Never, ever, EVER attempt to get the upper hand by using the pulpit to grind a public or private axe during your sermon. The preacher who fights from the pulpit against the congregation has lost his credibility as a preacher.

24. The preacher should look and speak as a designated representative of Jesus Christ. No need for a sophisticated approach – sincerity works perfectly.

Chapter Four • *The Preacher & His Preaching*

25. If it is your first time to preach – give yourself some pregame confidence. Consider going to the church the day before and see what it looks like to stand in the pulpit and look out on the (empty) pews. It is understandable that up until now, you have spent your entire life looking up at the rostrum from the pews.

26. Be prepared for Satan's attack. Understand that Satan is working overtime to interfere with your spiritual process. Ask the Savior to help you and He will be victorious through you. Remember your public ministry can do immense good for Christ if you don't let Satan's tool of despair overcome you.

Personal Reflection

- Rank your use of the four preaching styles. Which style interests you the most?

- How can I improve my preparation?

- Am I losing people while preaching? Am I clear on my thesis statement?

- What are some ways I can improve my delivery?

Discuss with your Pastor

- Constructive criticisms after you preach.

- Ways to improve upon your delivery.

- How to craft a sermon using one of the styles that you ranked '3' or '4'.

Chapter Five

THE PREACHER

HIS DEMONS

Preachers possess an inordinate and outrageous sense of grandeur. Often, many misguided preachers fall prey to believing themselves as demigods or God Junior. Young preachers must give heed to the fact that – contrary to popular belief – they are not the best thing since sliced bread.

The preacher must strive to remain humble. National Evangelist Dr. Manuel Scott, Jr. utilizes the acronym Edging God Out when looking at the word "ego." The preacher who does not have his ego in check will think more highly of themselves than of God and God's word. They will display a superiority complex by viewing the people of God as inferior creatures. The egotistical preacher will also possess a corrosive jealousy of any preacher who is well-known. Often, these preachers hold a perverted sense of entitlement believing that the world owes them something.

> *Dear Young Preacher,*
>
> *You are not called to be popular.*
> *You are called to be faithful.*

Chapter Five • *The Preacher & His Demons*

It is important to remember that no one can beat you at being you. The late Dr. Manuel Scott, Sr. encourages the young preacher to "wear your cuff links of humility and make sure they are shining."

For I say, through the grace given unto me, to every man that is among you, not to think of himself more highly than he ought to think; but to think soberly, according as God hath dealt to every man the measure of faith. (Romans 12:3 KJV)

And he said to them all, If any man will come after me, let him deny himself, and take up his cross daily, and follow me. (Luke 9:23 KJV)

For whosoever exalteth himself shall be abased; and he that humbleth himself shall be exalted. (Luke 14:11 KJV)

Pride goeth before destruction, and a haughty spirit before a fall. (Proverbs 16:18 KJV)

King Saul, Absalom, Samson, Pharoah and even Lucifer (Satan) fell prey to their egos.

And it came to pass as they came, when David was returned from the slaughter of the Philistine, that the women came out of all cities of Israel, singing and dancing, to meet king Saul, with tabrets, with joy, and with instruments of musick. And the women answered one another as they played, and said, Saul hath slain his thousands, and David his ten thousands. And Saul was very wroth, and the saying displeased him; and he said, They have ascribed unto David ten thousands, and to me they have ascribed but thousands: and what can he have more but the kingdom? And Saul eyed David from that day and forward. (I Samuel 18:6-9 KJV)

But Absalom sent spies throughout all the tribes of Israel, saying, As soon as ye hear the sound of the trumpet, then ye shall say, Absalom reigneth in Hebron. And with Absalom wen two hundred men out of Jerusalem, that were called; and they went in their simplicity, and they knew not any thing. And Absalom sent for Ahithophel the Gilonite, David's counsellor, from his city, even from Giloh, while he offered sacrifices. And the conspiracy was strong; for the people increased continually with Absalom. And there came a messenger to David, saying, The hearts of the men of Israel are after Absalom. And David said unto all his servants that were with him at Jerusalem, Arise, and let us flee; for we shall not else escape from Absalom: make speed to depart, lest he overtake us suddenly, and bring evil upon us, and smite the city with the edge of the sword. (II Samuel 15:10-14 KJV)

And it came to pass, when she pressed him daily with her words, and urged him, so that his soul was vexed unto death; That he told her all his heart, and said unto her, There hath not come a rasor upon mine head; for I have been a Nazarite unto God from my mother's womb: if I be shaven, then my strength will go from me, and I shall become weak, and be like any other man. And Delilah saw that he had told her all his heart, she sent and called for the lords of the Philistines, saying, Come up this once, for he hath shewed me all his heart. Then the lords of the Philistines came up unto her, and brought money in their hand. And she made him sleep upon her knees; and she called for a man, and she caused him to shave off the seven locks of his head; and she began to afflict him, and his strength went from him. And she said, The Philistines be upon thee, Samson. And he awoke out of his sleep, and said, I will go out as at other times before, and shake myself. And he wist not that the LORD was departed from him. (Judges 16:16-20 KJV)

And Pharoah said, Who is the LORD, that I should obey his voice to let Israel go? I know not the LORD, neither will I let Israel go. (Exodus 5:2 KJV)

How art thou fallen from heaven, O Lucifer, son of the morning! how art thou cut down to the ground, which didst weaken the

Chapter Five • The Preacher & His Demons

nations! For thou hast said in thine heart, I will ascend into heaven, I will exalt my throne above the stars of God: I will sit also upon the mount of the congregation, in the sides of the north: I will ascend above the heights of the clouds; I will be like the most High. (Isaiah 14:12-14 KJV)

And there was war in heaven: Michael and his angels fought against the dragon; and the dragon fought and his angels, And prevailed not; neither was their place found any more in heaven. And the great dragon was cast out, that old serpent, called the devil, and Satan, which deceiveth the whole world: he was cast out into the earth, and his angels were cast out with him. (Revelations 12:7-9 KJV)

And he said unto them, I beheld Satan as lightning fall from heaven. (Luke 10:18 KJV)

Dr. Sigmund Freud, father of psychoanalysis, used the term libido to describe the human sex drive. It is an ecclesiastical ludicrous phenomenon that, in this highly sex-saturated society, we have so many scandalous preachers (majority imitating bad role models) who prostitute the ministry by trying to be players, ballers, whoremongers, homosexuals and bisexuals. Sadly, we are experiencing a generation of preachers who possess the eloquence of a Demosthenes and a Cicero but, the morals of an alley cat!

Charles Haddon Spurgeon says that the preacher who has not been called to Holy living has not been called to the ministry. This demon of sexual immorality has plagued the men of God for some time now. Even Dr. Martin Luther King, Jr. reportedly said that he did not know one black Baptist preacher who was faithful to his wife. The four-headed dragon of mistresses, pornography, bisexuality, and liquor are devouring preachers, especially young preachers, at warp-like speed. If the young preacher fails to control this demon of their libido, they are doomed to suffer the fate of having their preaching power dissipated over time to zero.

A Charge to Preach: *Letters to A Young Preacher*

I beseech you therefore, brethren, by the mercies of God, that ye present your bodies a living sacrifice, holy, acceptable unto God, which is your reasonable service. And be not conformed to this world: but be ye transformed by the renewing of your mind, that ye may prove what is that good, and acceptable, and perfect, will of God. (Romans 12:1-2 KJV)

What? know ye not that your body is the temple of the Holy Ghost which is in you, which ye have of God, and ye are not your own? For ye are bought with a price: therefore glorify God in your body, and in your spirit, which are God's. (I Corinthians 6:19-20 KJV)

Watch and pray, that ye enter not into temptation: the spirit indeed is willing, but the flesh is weak. (Matthew 26:41 KJV)

Dear Young Preacher,

C.S. Lewis wrote "As long as you are proud, you cannot know God. A proud man is always looking down on things and people and of course, as long as you are looking down, you cannot see something that is above you."

Take care to bring your body under subjection daily so that you may make full proof of your ministry, effectively winning souls for the kingdom! Remember the words of Dr. Manuel Scott, Sr. that it is "an irreconcilable contradiction when a Christian minister acts as though certain passages are not in the Bible."

There is also the demon we know as "Mammon" which is the Syriac and Aramaic word for money and/or material things. The reason it has become such a demon is because far too many preachers (heavily influenced by who they see on television or YouTube) are chasing the dollar bill rather than diligently seeking the Lord's will for their lives in ministry. Instead of surrendering to the high calling of service, many preachers are caught up in bling-bling (materialism on steroids).

According to the late Dr. Manuel Scott, Sr., there exists this problem that contemporary church today pays more attention to the lost coin as opposed to the lost sheep. There is nothing inherently wrong with the preacher having nice things if those things do not have the preacher. Bishop Charles Blake has said that many preachers need to be careful bragging about their class cars, houses, jewelry, websites, networking, etc. because that is not what God has called us into the Ministry for. It is especially important during this season of the prosperity blitz and blasphemy for the young preacher to recall the astute warning of Jesus in Matthew 16:26.

For what is a man profited, if he shall gain the whole word, and lose his own soul: or what shall a man give in exchange for his soul? (KJV)

No man can serve two masters: for either he will hate the one, and love the other; or else he will hold to the one, and despise the other. Ye cannot serve God and mammon. (Matthew 6:24 KJV)

A bishop then must be blameless, the husband of one wife, vigilant, sober, of good behaviour, given to hospitality, apt to teach; Not given to wine, no striker, not greedy of filthy lucre; but patient, not a brawler, not covetous; (I Timothy 3:2-3 KJV)

But they that will be rich fall into temptation and a snare, and into many foolish and hurtful lusts, which drown men in destruction and perdition. For the love of money is the root of all evil: which while some coveted after, they have erred from the faith, and pierced themselves with many sorrows. (I Timothy 6:9-10 KJV)

> Dear Young Preacher,
>
> Abraham Joshua Heschel wrote "God is of no importance unless God is of supreme importance." God will not take the back burner to anything or anyone you attempt to place ahead of him.

The preacher's call to the Ministry is to preach truth to power and not popular anecdotes and cliches which have no Scriptural foundation. Sure, the people may give you more to make them feel good but a word of caution – the penalty for not sounding the warning of destruction will be far worse as opposed to you sounding the alarm and the people refusing to adhere.

There are essentially three ways the preacher can handle these three demons:

1. Cogitation
2. Associations
3. Situations

Cogitation refers to how and what the preacher thinks. First and foremost, preachers should never think of themselves more highly than they ought to think (c.f. Romans 12:3; Luke 14:11; Proverbs 16:18). Preachers should intentionally park their minds on thoughts that are healthy, edifying, proactive, and positive in every way.

> Dear Young Preacher,
>
> Leave the pornography alone!

Chapter Five • The Preacher & His Demons

The preacher must realize that the mind is a muscle, and the more you exercise it, by way of reading, serious thinking, and good conversation, the stronger and sharper the mind becomes. The preacher, in particular the young preacher, should also recognize that the mind is a sponge that will virtually soak up any image (good or bad) that is placed before it. Never forget that while education does not give you the anointing, it does sharpen the anointing. God can best use a sharpened tool for the work of Ministry.

Let this mind be in you, which was also in Christ Jesus: (Philippians 2:5 KJV)

Finally, brethren, whatsoever things are true, whatsoever things are honest, whatsoever things are just, whatsoever things are pure, whatsoever things are lovely, whatsoever things are of good report; if there be any virtue, and if there be any praise, think on these things. (Philippians 4:8 KJV)

For to be carnally minded is death; but to be spiritually minded is life and peace. Because the carnal mind is enmity against God, neither indeed can be. So then they that are in the flesh cannot please God. (Romans 8:6-8 KJV)

Most preachers, especially young preachers, begin their downward slide by associating with other preachers who are demonically negative and satanically worldly (c.f. Proverbs 13:20; 4:14; 24:1). Preachers must correctly discern protein people (make you strong) from kryptonite people (make you weak).

Let us therefore follow after the things which make for peace, and things wherewith one may edify another. (Romans 14:19 KJV)

Wisdom strengtheneth the wise more than ten mighty men which are in the city. (Ecclesiastes 7:19 KJV)

But I have prayed for thee, that thy faith fail not: and when thou art converted, strengthen thy brethren. (Luke 22:32 KJV)

It is imperative that the preacher have an intimate association with the Holy Spirit! For when the Holy Spirit is controlling the preacher, the preacher's life is in order. When the Holy Spirit is not controlling the preacher, his life is out of order.

> *Dear Young Preacher,*
>
> *One of the best ways to determine and discern if you should associate yourself with a certain preacher, is to see how well they measure up to the Fruit of the Spirit.*

But the fruit of the Spirit is love, joy, peace, longsuffering, gentleness, goodness, faith, Meekness, temperance: against such there is no law. (Galatians 5:22-23 KJV)

> *Dear Young Preacher,*
>
> *You must realize that while some people may still be in your heart (particularly old friends or acquaintances), they do not belong in your future.*

Be ye not unequally yoked together with unbelievers: for what fellowship hath righteousness with unrighteousness? and what communion hath light with darkness? (II Corinthians 6:14 KJV)

He that walketh with wise men shall be wise: but a companion of fools shall be destroyed. (Proverbs 13:20 KJV)

I am a companion of all them that fear thee, and of them that keep thy precepts. (Psalm 119:63 KJV)

And be not drunk with wine, wherein is excess; but be filled with the Spirit; (Ephesians 5:18 KJV)

Chapter Five • The Preacher & His Demons

But ye are not in the flesh, but in the Spirit, if so be that the Spirit of God dwell in you. Now if any man have not the Spirit of Christ, he is none of his. (Romans 8:9 KJV)

The Spirit of the Lord is upon me, because he hath anointed me to preach the gospel to the poor; he hath sent me to heal the brokenhearted, to preach deliverance to the captives, and recovering of sight to the blind, to set at liberty them that are bruised. (Luke 4:18 KJV)

Much of the preacher's moral demise has to do with situations and locations they allow themselves to be placed in. Preachers, especially young preachers, would do well to guard where they allow themselves to be seen and identified with. Put simply, when it comes to the preacher's reputation and credibility, their physical location makes all the difference! Night clubs, strip joints, liquor bars, casinos, drugs, pornography, and questionable company should be avoided like the plague!

> *Dear Young Preachers,*
>
> *When it comes to the issue of where you permit yourself to go and be seen, always remember that church people are ubiquitous, that is, they are everywhere, and will most certainly report to others what they have seen.*

The steps of a good man are ordered by the LORD: *and he delighteth in his way.* (Psalm 37:23 KJV)

My son, walk not thou in the way with them; refrain thy foot from their path: For their feet run to evil, and make haste to shed blood. (Proverbs 1:15-16 KJV)

Abstain from all appearance of evil. (I Thessalonians 5:22 KJV)

These six things doth the Lord hate: yea, seven are an abomination unto him: A proud look, a lying tongue, and hands that shed innocent blood, A heart that deviseth wicked imaginations, feet that be swift in running to mischief. (Proverbs 6:16-18 KJV)

Personal Reflection

- Identify your personal demons. How are you dealing with them? Are you dealing with them?

- Are my sexual desires in check or do I need help dealing with them?

- What relationships do I have that may be of detriment to my ministry?

Discuss with your Pastor

- Those demons that you are struggling with and what resources are available to help you handle them.

- Your personal relationships – inside and outside the church. Are there any associations adversely affecting your Ministry (or possibly in the future)?

Chapter Six
PRACTICAL INSTRUCTIONS *for* THE YOUNG PREACHER

1. Before you tell your pastor that you have been called to preach, let them see that you have been called to Sunday School, Bible Study, Prayer Meeting and Tithing!

2. Ministry has changed tremendously over time – some good, some bad. However, it is imperative that we uphold a good and godly standard as we represent the kingdom of God. We may not be perfect, but we should strive for perfection daily.

3. Maintain respect for seasoned sages. The student is no better than the teacher. He licensed you. He ordained you. He shared his pulpit with you. He nurtured you. So, honor him.

4. Maintain preaching integrity. If you don't believe it, don't preach it. Never put on to draw a crowd. The gospel that we have been entrusted to carry is too precious and important.

5. Be authentic. There's only one you. I have non-denominational friends, Apostolic friends, Full Gospel Baptist friends and COGIC friends, but I am unapologetically Baptist to my core. Be who you are and know what you believe!

Chapter Six • *Practical Instructions for the Young Preacher*

6. Study. Don't recycle sermons or try to pass off another preacher's sermon as your own. If you wait until you're invited to preach, to prepare to preach – you will never be ready to preach. "Down time" is prep time.

7. Dress presentably. There's nothing wrong with looking like a preacher. You are a preacher, right? People see you before they hear you. Doctors wear scrubs. Lawyers wear suits. Soldiers wear uniforms. Preachers should present like preachers.

8. Don't be envious. Jealousy doesn't become the clergy. You're the biggest you there will ever be. Water your own garden and watch it grow.

9. Be sure that your "criticisms" of other preachers come from a genuine place of concern or righteous indignation – and not from a dark place of jealousy or insecurity. A bitter minister is of no help to anyone.

10. The "points" you develop during sermon preparation should flow naturally from the passage you are preaching. Sometimes the passage yields itself to one or two points; and sometimes three or four. The goal is not being clever but being guided by the Holy Spirit toward an end of being faithful in our dealing with the Word of God.

11. People may have their preference of teachers, but there is no preference of message. Regardless of your style of teaching, ALL proclaimers for Christ have the same message – the gospel. When THE GOSPEL is faithfully proclaimed, it translates to EVERY demographic, ethnicity, culture, and status in spite of who articulates it or how it's articulated. Keep your unique style, but never ditch the message.

12. Applying a sound hermeneutical method to biblical interpretation is good just don't abandon it when you get to passages that seem to favor a view that you have a vested interest in believing.

13. EVERY sermon you preach should be doctrinal.

14. Value Preparation before proclamation. Study the text (in context of the immediate text) before you shout them under the pew on Sunday.

15. Don't let the crowd control the truth.

16. Steven Lawson says there are only two types of preachers: 1) those who preach the Bible and 2) those who need to resign.

17. Unless you are invited/beckoned for, any seat in the sanctuary is ok. You don't have to be in the pulpit or on the front row, especially if you are late.

18. There's no room for selfishness in ministry. We are called to pour it all out.

19. Love people. Serve people. Give 100%. But always remember that you're called by God and kept by God; thus, you're accountable first and foremost to Him.

20. You don't have to wait until Easter Sunday to proclaim the death & resurrection of Jesus Christ. It is the Gospel message that makes the distinction between preaching and motivational speaking.

21. The Bible is more interesting that ANYTHING you have to say!

22. In every date with delivery, the preacher should be eager and expectant for some act of repentance. The sermon can never be exclusively informative. It must be persuasive!

23. Jesus is referred to many things in the Bible but nowhere in the scriptures is he identified as being alright. He is more than Alright!

24. One sure way for the preacher to know he is on point and that is to do what he is supposed to do. Rather it's read, pray, sing, preach or even deliver encouraging words, the preacher must learn to do what he has been tasked to do and return to his seat.

25. Any preacher is playing a fatally short-sighted game who sounds off on the Christian theology and neglects the Christian ethics. The preacher is as much and ethician as he is a theologian.

26. If you are going to preach (or speak) well to the people to whom you are sent, you must speak first with the one who sends you.

27. Adequate preparation for the preacher is twofold: the preparation of the message, and preparation of the man.

28. If it is your task to say a word for God and about God, it is prudent for you to habitually speak with God.

29. A mere 'three *S* preacher' – a stomper, spitter, and a sweater – is neither necessary nor desirable.

30. It is part of the pulpiteer's burden that he is called upon to make full proof of his proclamation and his ministry in a God-rejecting society.

31. When a person talks from his head, the people look at him; when he talks from his heart, the people listen to him; when he talks from his emotions, the people feel him; and when he talks from all three, the people believe him.

32. Preaching and pride just do not go together. They are as incompatible as preaching and prayerlessness.

33. When asked to preach a sermon for a particular occasion (Father's Day, Mother's Day, Youth Day, Men's Day, etc.), do as you have been asked. If you wish not to preach a sermon specifically for that occasion, it is best that you do not accept the invitation.

34. Preachers should dress like preachers and prophets, not like pimps and pushers.

35. When preaching, always remember to 'Make it plain!' When you stand to preach, your task is to make the sermon relatable and understood by all who hear.

36. Never use the pulpit as your personal weapon to try to get YOUR point across. Your job as a preacher is to pull the souls of the people from the pits of Hell.

37. When a preacher is trying out for a church, he is dealing with two unpredictable: God and the people.

38. A sermon ought to have portability. It ought to be portable. That is, you ought to be able to take something that was said in the sermon with you.

39. To be a great preacher or pastor, you must first be a great person.

40. Preaching is reporting on what one knows about God.

Chapter Six • *Practical Instructions for the Young Preacher*

41. The gospel preacher has the task of getting others to see what he sees. If you don't see anything, you ought not say anything.

42. We who preach the gospel must be the gospel. We must live it as well as speak it. If you are not going to live it, don't you dare preach it!

43. While you are learning to preach, also learn to be a preacher. You don't know how many people will be holding onto you because they believe you are holding onto God. So, tighten your grip on Him.

44. No matter how much you know, if you do not know God, you don't know enough. We must search God out and come to know Him so we can speak of Him. Do you ever ask: What did God think of my sermon? While you are making the people glad, are you making God mad?

45. Preach the word, believe what you preach, and live what you preach.

46. If you're going to preach, don't sing. If you're going to sing, preach first.

47. You never want to have a gospel that you can only preach on one side of town.

48. The late Dr. E. K. Bailey said, "The hour of examination is not the hour of preparation." The preacher cannot wait until the Hymn of Preparation to find a sermon to preach to God's people who are anxiously anticipating a word from the Lord.

Personal Reflection

- What three (3) instructions do I most agree with? Is my ministry the better because of it?

- What is one piece of advice I can share with other young preachers that is not listed?

- Have I – knowing or unknowingly – done any of these things as a preacher that I should not have? What correction action will be taken?

Discuss with your Pastor

- Things he has learned through his years of ministry.

Chapter Seven
To Pastor

or

not to Pastor...

THAT IS THE QUESTION!

Due to the tremendous influence of black Baptist tradition, most preachers automatically equate the call to preach as the call to the pastorate. It is important for the young preacher to know and understand that the kingdom has a dire need for ministries other than the pastorate: Evangelism, Military Chaplaincy, Christian Education, Hospital/Prison Ministries, Youth and Young Adult Ministries, Media Ministry, Suicide Prevention, etc. Young preachers should prayerfully consider Ephesians 4:11-12.

And he gave some, apostles; and some, prophets; and some, evangelists; and some, pastors and teachers; for the perfecting of the saints, for the work of the ministry, for the edifying of the body of Christ. [KJV]

In view of the need for ministers in such critical areas in addition to the pastorate, the minister that is truly convinced that they are being called to the pastorate must seriously prepare themselves for

Chapter Seven • *To Pastor or not to Pastor...That is the Question!*

such an undertaking by waiting their turn. Put simply, as an Associate Minister to your Pastor, you should patiently demonstrate consistent, helpful, and true allegiance to your Pastor until God calls you to be a Pastor. It is essential to note that the Bible is clear that if the young preacher would just wait their turn, everything will work out alright.

And let us not grow weary while doing good, for in due season we shall reap if we do not lose heart. [Galatians 6:9 NKJV]

Therefore, my beloved brethren, be steadfast, immovable, always abounding in the work of the Lord, knowing that your labor is not in vain in the Lord. [I Corinthians 15:58 NKJV]

And we know that all things work together for good to those who love God, to those who are the called according to His purpose. [Romans 8:28 NKJV]

Even the youths shall faint and be weary, and the young men shall utterly fall, But those who wait on the Lord shall renew their strength; They shall mount up with wings like eagles, they shall run and not be weary, They shall walk and not faint. [Isaiah 40:30-31 NKJV]

For His anger is but for a moment, His favor is for life; Weeping may endure for a night, But joy comes in the morning. [Psalm 30:5 NKJV]

I waited patiently for the LORD; and He inclined to me, And heard my cry. He also brought me up out of a horrible pit, out of the miry clay, and set my feet upon a rock, and established my steps. He has put a new song in my mouth – Praise to our God; many will see it and fear, and will trust in the LORD. [Psalm 40:1-3 NKJV]

If God has truly called you to preach, and if you remain humble, you will get your turn to do great things in the Pastorate. With your patience and diligent preparation (college, seminary, etc.), God will provide opportunities for you to preach, to teach, and if it is His Will, to eventually pastor.

A man's gift makes room for him, and brings him before great men. [Proverbs 18:16 NKJV]

Always remember young preacher that there is always a Jehovah-Jireh (a God who will provide) in your future (c.f. Genesis 22:11-14).

Realize and recognize this, that God is going to advance your ministry according to His time schedule, not yours! Never try to compare the progress of your ministry with the progress of the ministry of other preachers. God's timing is "preacher-specific"; for only in His own time will He specifically deal with YOU and your ministry. Remember that God's sovereign timing is wiser than your desires, wiser than your ambition, wiser than your friends and relatives, and wiser than any strategy of self-promotion. When you wait on His timing, you are waiting on a perfect blessing (c.f. Galatians 4:4; 6:9).

No matter the desired ministry, it is important to remember the call is to serve!

And it will be said in that day: "Behold, this is our God; we have waited for Him, and He will save us. This is the LORD*; we have waited for Him; we will be glad and rejoice in His salvation."* [Isaiah 25:9 NKJV]

But let patience have its perfect work, that you may be perfect and complete, lacking nothing. [James 1:4 NKJV]

It is painstakingly apparent that many young preachers have difficulty waiting for their shot. Many young preachers possess oversized egos believing that they can do a better job than their Pastor

Chapter Seven • *To Pastor or not to Pastor...That is the Question!*

(c.f. Proverbs 16:18). Some have an undersized sense of togetherness based on their commitment to being honest, moral, dependable, and loyal. See Matthew 26:74-75 and John 4:24. For some young ministers, they have a self-destructive un-coachable and narcissistic demeanor. They outright detest any type of authority because they [think they] know everything (c.f. Proverbs 12:15).

Unfortunately, many of these young preachers fall prey to allowing disgruntled members to have them foolishly believe that their pastor is deliberately attempting to hold them back (I John 4:1). They generally are glory and glamour addicts believing that they must constantly be in the limelight.

Let your light so shine before men, that they may see your good works and glorify your Father in heaven. [Matthew 5:16 NKJV]

For you were bought at a price; therefore glorify God in your body and in your spirit, which are God's. [I Corinthians 6:20 NKJV]

For we do not preach ourselves, but Christ Jesus the Lord, and ourselves your bondservants for Jesus' sake. [II Corinthians 2:5 NKJV]

Some young preachers reject the concept of the pay your dues principle. They do not have the foggiest notion of the costs that Pastors have paid and continue to pay to lead the people of God. Understand that Pastors have given unlimited amounts of time, sacrifice and money while serving – and at the same time suffering criticism, betrayal, and family neglect.

Are they ministers of Christ? – I speak as a fool – I am more: in labors more abundant, in stripes above measure, in prisons more frequently, in deaths often. From the Jews five times I received forty stripes minus one. Three times I was beaten with rods; once I was stoned; three times I was shipwrecked; a night and a day I have been in the deep; in journeys often, in perils of waters, in perils of robbers, in perils of my own countrymen, in perils of the Gentiles, in perils in the city, in perils in the wilderness, in perils in the sea, in perils among false brethren; in weariness and toil, in sleeplessness often, in hunger and thirst, in fastings often, in cold and nakedness – besides the other things, what comes upon me daily: my deep concern for all the churches. [II Corinthians 23-28 NKJV]

But the Lord said to him, "God, for he is a chosen vessel of Mine to bear My name before Gentiles, kings, and the children of Israel. For I will show him how many things he must suffer for My name's sake." [Acts 9:15-16 NKJV]

My brethren, take the prophets, who spoke in the name of the Lord, as an example of suffering and patience. [James 5:10 NKJV]

And everyone who has left houses or brothers or sisters or father or mother or wife or children or lands, for My name's sake, shall receive a hundredfold, and inherit eternal life. [Matthew 19:29 NKJV]

It is prudent for the young preacher to come to terms with the biblical truth that God still gives churches Pastors (Jeremiah 3:15). Knowing this should help you realize that your Pastor has been placed where he is by God Himself (Acts 20:28). Prepare yourself academically by attending an accredited University, Bible College and/or Seminary if you truly wish to Pastor. Remember that the future belongs to those who are prepared. While God can use any tool, He best can use a sharpened tool!

Be diligent to present yourself approved to God, a worker who does not need to be ashamed, rightly dividing the word of truth. [II Timothy 2:15 NKJV]

My people are destroyed for lack of knowledge. Because you have rejected knowledge, I also will reject you from being priest for Me;

Chapter Seven • To Pastor or not to Pastor...That is the Question!

because you have forgotten the law of your God, I also will forget your children. [Hosea 4:6 NKJV]

But grow in the grace and knowledge of our Lord and Savior Jesus Christ. To Him be the glory both now and forever. Amen. [II Peter 3:18 NKJV]

Carefully observe the right and spiritual things your Pastor does. Learn how to praise and diplomatically defend your Pastor in public. Distance yourself from church cliques, complainers, gossipers, and known "enemies" of the Pastor.

Be kindly affectionate to one another with brotherly love, in honor giving preference to one another. [Romans 12:10 NKJV]

Let the elders who rule well be counted worthy of double honor, especially those who labor in the word and doctrine. [I Timothy 5:17 NKJV]

It is undoubtedly necessary for the young preacher who hopes to enter the pastorate to carefully examine yourself considering the qualifications stipulated in I Timothy 3:1-7.

This is a true saying, If a man desire the office of a bishop, he desireth a good work. A bishop then must be blameless, the husband of one wife, vigilant, sober, of good behaviour, given to hospitality, apt to teach; Not given to wine, no striker, not greedy of filthy lucre; but patient, not a brawler, not covetous; One that ruleth well his own house, having his children in subjection with all gravity; (For if a man know not how to rule his own house, how shall he take care of the church of God?) Not a novice, lest being lifted up with pride he fall into condemnation of the devil. Moreover he must have a good report of them which are without; lest he fall into reproach and the snare of the devil. [KJV]

Preacher, are you blameless? The Greek word is *anepileptos* and means "not open to attack"; irreproachable. It refers to a prospective pastor whose character is impeccable. If so, you may make a good pastor.

Preacher, are you apt to teach? Do you have the temperament and skill to teach God's Word? If so, you may make a good pastor.

Preacher, are you greedy for filthy lucre? That is, are you money-hungry? If so, you will not make a good pastor.

Preacher, do you rule your own house well? Do you have your household, especially your children, under control? If so, you may make a good pastor.

Preacher, do you have a good report of them which are without? Do you have a good reputation among non-believers? If so, you may make a good pastor.

Nevertheless, whatever ministry you feel God is calling you, take time and get to know your Bible thoroughly.

But his delight is in the law of the LORD, and in His law he meditates day and night. [Psalm 1:2 NKJV]

You search the Scriptures, for in them you think you have eternal life; and these are they which testify of Me. [John 5:39 NKJV]

As newborn babes, desire the pure milk of the word, that you may grow thereby [I Peter 2:2 NKJV]

Jesus answered and said to them, "You are mistaken, not knowing the Scriptures nor the power of God." [Matthew 22:29 NKJV]

Chapter Seven • *To Pastor or not to Pastor...That is the Question!*

Personal Reflection

- Do I feel that I am being called to Pastor?

- Is the call to Pastor coming from the Lord, the church, or myself?

- What qualifies me to be a Pastor?

Discuss with your Pastor

- Why you feel you are being called to Pastor?

- How to candidate for a church.

- Your perception of a Pastor's role.

Chapter Eight

THE PREACHER

HIS GIFTS

Dear Young Preacher,

There are many different ministries that exist within the church.

Sadly, too often a call to ministry has been incorrectly considered a called to preach. Possibly, this is due to a lack of understanding that the call to ministry is a call to serve. Dr. Charles V. Bryant identifies thirty-two (32) gifts that are existent in the church.

It is crucial that the preacher understand that these gifts are for service as opposed to personal status, power, or popularity. They enable us to do effective service for the body of Christ, the church and, - through the church – the world. Gifts are neither personal property nor natural qualities for the preacher to use as he wishes. They are divine energy which creates, molds, and directs new abilities for special ministries to the world through the church.

As every man hath received the gift, even so minister the same one to another, as good stewards of the manifold grace of God. If any man speak, let him speak as the oracles of God; if any man minister, let him do it as of the ability which God giveth: that God in all things may be glorified through Jesus Christ, to whom be praise and dominion for ever and ever. Amen. (I Peter 4:10-11 KJV)

But the manifestation of the Spirit is given to every man to profit withal. (I Corinthians 12:7 KJV)

For the perfecting of the saints for the work of the ministry, for the edifying of the body of Christ: (Ephesians 4:12 KJV)

Understanding that these gifts are for service helps us to accept the fact that God assigns and empowers the gifts. Wanting certain gifts does not guarantee their acquisition by the believer. The believer has no control over the gift or gifts that God assigns. It is God himself who knows what is needed for the edification of the body of Christ and the common good of the church.

But covet earnestly the best gifts: and yet shew I unto you a more excellent way. (I Corinthians 12:31 KJV)

Having then gifts differing according to the grace that is given to us, whether prophecy, let us prophesy according to the proportion of faith; (Romans 12:6 KJV)

And there are diversities of operations, but it is the same God which worketh all in all. But the manifestation of the Spirit is given to every man to profit withal. (I Corinthians 12:6-7 KJV)

Take note that every Christian believer has been gifted for special ministries. Those who say they have not do err inadvertently equating gifts with talents or natural abilities. Unfortunately, many excuse themselves from serving in the church claiming the absence of any usable talents or skills. However, the biblical truth is that all Christians possess spiritual gifts that carry extraordinary powers and responsibilities.

Dr. Bryant asserts that the limit to the variety of gifts can only be known by God. According to Ephesians, the purpose of the gifts is to bring the church to full maturity in Christ. This cannot take place among disconnected individuals or within a corporate body that overlooks the welfare and participation of its members. Every part of the body is intricately, intimately, and vitally connected with Christ as head.

Nay, much more those members of the body, which seem to be more feeble, are necessary: And those members of the body, which we think to be less honourable, upon these we bestow more abundant honour; and our uncomely parts have more abundant comeliness. For our comely parts have no need: but God hath tempered the body together, having given more abundant honour to that part which lacked: That there should be no schism in the body; but that the members should have the same care one for another. (I Corinthians 12:22-25 KJV)

It is also important to note that health and growth can be determined by the use of gifts. Remember, the church is a single organism composed of many unique parts. The health of the whole body is dependent on the health and proper functioning of the individual parts. Therefore, the body must not neglect or discount the position or function of any organ – no matter its size or distance from the head. Likewise, no individual part should overlook the value of the whole body.

And he gave some, apostles; and some, prophets; and some, evangelists; and some, pastors and teachers; For the perfecting of the saints for the work of the ministry, for the edifying of the body of Christ: Till we all come in the unity of the faith, and of the knowledge of the Son of God, unto a perfect man, unto the measure of the stature of the fulness of Christ: That we henceforth be no more children, tossed to and fro, and carried about with every wind of doctrine, by the sleight of men, and cunning craftiness, whereby they lie in wait to deceive; But speaking the truth in love, may grow up unto him in all things, which is the head, even Christ: From whom the whole body fitly joined together and compacted by that which every joint supplieth, according to the effectual working in the measure of every part, maketh increase of the body unto the edifying of itself in love. (Ephesians 4:11-16 KJV)

Chapter Eight • *The Preacher & His Gifts*

Due to some misunderstandings about the gifts, it is important that the preacher know and understand what these gifts are not. Spiritual Gifts are not: (1) acquired skills nor natural talents; (2) roles; (3) offices in the church; (4) the Fruit of the Spirit; (5) for self-gain; (6) divisive; or (7) the same for everyone.

However, these manifestations of the spirit are: (1) unmerited blessings from God; (2) job descriptions for ministries; (3) a means for discovering God's will; (4) guarantees of effective service; (5) a means to efficient service; (6) securities for health and growth; (7) the revealed presence of the living Christ; and (8) the guarantor of lasting results.

The preacher would do well to be able to identify such manifestations of the Holy Spirit in operation today. While several spiritual gifts inventories are available online, one is also provided in the appendix that examines the thirty-two gifts recognized by Dr. Bryant. These gifts are defined here.

1. *Prophecy.* The ability to link biblical truths and God's will for today's living and to be an instrument for revealing or interpreting historic or current messages from God for righteous and just living in today's world.

    Acts 2:14-36; 11:28; 15:32; 21:10; 21:9-11
    Romans 12:6
    I Corinthians 12:10; 14:3, 6, 24
    Ephesians 3:1-6; 4:11-14

2. *Pastor.* The ability to carry varieties of spiritual, physical, and social concerns for groups and individuals and to persist over long periods of time and circumstances with effective caring.

    Matthew 18:12-14   *Ephesians 4:11-14*
    John 10:1-30   *I Timothy 3:1-7*
    Acts 20:28   *I Peter 5:2-4*

3. *Teaching.* The ability to discern, analyze, and deliver biblical and other spiritual truths to help others to comprehend and accept the clear calling of God to live justly and righteously.

   Acts 13:1, 18:24-28;   *I Timothy 2:7*
   20:20-21   *II Timothy 1:11*
   I Corinthians 12:28   *James 3:1*
   Ephesians 4:11

4. *Wisdom.* The ability to make concrete, practical, and specific applications of divine knowledge received directly from God, from one's spiritual gift of knowledge, or from another's shared gift of gifts.

   Acts 6:3, 10; 7:10   *Colossians 1:28; 3:16*
   I Corinthians 1:18-27;   *II Peter 3:15*
   3:18-19; 12:18

5. *Knowledge.* The ability to ascertain and to understand the universal and timeless truths of God and to link them with the church in its mission through Christ for justice and righteousness in the world.

   Acts 5:1-11   *II Corinthians 11:6*
   Romans 11:33   *Ephesians 3:19*
   I Corinthians 12:8   *Colossians 2:3*

6. *Exhortation.* The ability to counsel, inspire, motivate, encourage, and strengthen others in and through their efforts to live out God's will and calling as Christians in pain or pleasure, want or plenty.

   Acts 4:36; 11:19-26;   *I Thessalonians 2:11*
   14:22   *I Timothy 4:13*
   Romans 12:8   *Hebrews 10:25*

Chapter Eight • *The Preacher & His Gifts*

7. *Discerning of Spirits*. The ability to differentiate between good and evil, right, and wrong, and what is of God, human nature, or evil, and to use this knowledge for the protection and health of the body of Christ.

   Matthew 7:6 *II Peter 2:1-3*
   Acts 5:1-11; 8:22-23 *I John 4:1-6*
   I Corinthians 12:10

8. *Giving*. The ability to manage one's resources of income, time, energy, and skills to exceed what is a reasonable standard for giving to the church, an amount that brings joy and power to do more for further service.

   I Kings 17:8-16 *Acts 4:32-37*
   Mark 12:41-44 *Romans 12:8*
   Luke 8:1-3; 21:1-4 *II Corinthians 8:1-7*

9. *Helps*. The ability and eagerness to aid or assist others in need to such an extent that the helper receives as much as the persons helped.

   Psalm 21:1 *Acts 9:36*
   Mark 15:41 *Romans 16:1-2*
   Luke 8:2-3 *I Corinthians 12:28*

10. *Mercy*. The ability to identify with and feel the physical, mental, spiritual, and emotional pain or distress of others and to feel the absolute necessity to do something to relieve them.

    Matthew 20:29-34 *Acts 11:28-30; 16:33-34*
    Mark 9:41 *Romans 12:8*
    Luke 10:33-35

11. *Missionary.* The ability to go beyond race, culture, subculture, creeds, nationality, or lifestyle to serve the basic human and spiritual needs of certain neglected peoples.

   Matthew 25:37-40;   *Romans 10:14-17*
   28:19-20   *I Corinthians 9:19-23*
   Acts 8:4-8; 13:2-12

12. *Evangelism.* The ability to give such a persuasive witness to the love of God as expressed in Jesus Christ that it moves others to accept that love and to become disciples of Christ.

   Acts 8:5-6   *I Timothy 2:7*
   I Corinthians 3:5-6   *II Timothy 4:5*
   Ephesians 4:11

13. *Hospitality.* The ability to extend caring and sharing to persons (strangers) beyond one's intimate circle to demonstrate and establish the unlimited and inclusive companionship of Christ.

   Matthew 25:35   *I Timothy 3:2*
   Acts 16:14-16   *Titus 1:8*
   Romans 12:13   *I Peter 4:9-10*

14. *Faith.* The ability to extend one's basic or saving faith to serve corporate or individual needs specifically related to the life and ministry of the church, the body of Christ.

   Matthew 17:19-21   *Romans 4:18-21*
   Mark 9:23   *I Corinthians 12:9*
   Acts 11:22-24   *Hebrews 11*

15. *Leadership.* The ability to envision God's will and purpose for the church and to demonstrate compelling skills in capturing

the imaginations, energies, skills, and spiritual gifts of others to pursue and accomplish God's will.

Luke 10:16
Acts 7:10
Romans 12:8

I Timothy 3:4; 5:17
Titus 3:8, 14
Hebrews 13:17

16. *Administration.* The ability to sort out resources and persons for effective church ministries and to organize and implement them into ministry projects until completion with eventful results.

Luke 14:28-30
Acts 6:1-7

Romans 12:8
I Corinthians 12:28

17. *Suffering.* The ability to endure hardship, pain, and distress with an amount of joy and fortitude to inspire others to endure their suffering and to lead others to accept God's offer of salvation made possible in Christ's suffering.

Matthew 16:24
Mark 8:34
John 18:11
Romans 8:17

II Corinthians 11:23-27; 12:1-10
Philippians 1:29
I Peter 4:12-14

18. *Healings.* The ability to cure or to be cured of ill conditions that hinder effective ministries for Christ, the church, or individuals.

Luke 5:17; 6:19; 9:2, 11, 42
Acts 3:1-10; 5:12-16

I Corinthians 12:9, 28
I Peter 2:24

19. *Prayer-Praise Language.* The ability to pray or to praise God with beneficial wordless phrases or utterances not familiar as a known language, and with such a joy-filled intimacy with

Christ that faith is strengthened, and ministries become effective.

Acts 2:1-13; 10:44-46; *Ephesians 6:18*
19:1-7 *I Corinthians 12:10, 28;*
Romans 8:26-27 *13:1; 14:4-5, 22*

20. *Interpretation.* The ability to hear, comprehend, and translate spiritual messages given by others in wordless phrases or utterances unfamiliar as a known language or to decipher and translate spiritual messages from another who speaks in a known language but not recognized by the interpreter.

Luke 24:27 *I Corinthians 12:10, 30;*
Acts 2:14-21 *14:5, 13, 27*

21. *Apostle.* The ability to adhere to the personality of Jesus Christ and his tradition of missional itinerancy so that one may wield effective spiritual oversight of new people in new places for the purpose of extending Christian ministries for spiritual, just, and righteous living.

Acts 15:1-2 *Galatians 2:1-10*
I Corinthians 12:28 *Ephesians 3:1-13; 4:11*
II Corinthians 12:12

22. *Singleness.* The ability to offer God and the church a life free from marriage, family responsibilities, and sexual frustrations to spend time and energies necessary for certain Christian ministries.

Isaiah 56:3-5 *I Corinthians 7:7, 27-28,*
Matthew 19:10-12; *32-35*
22:27-30

Chapter Eight • *The Preacher & His Gifts*

23. *Intercessory Prayer.* The ability to know when, and for whom or what to pray with effective results.

    Luke 22:41-44
    Acts 12:5, 12; 16:25-26
    Romans 8:26-27

    Colossians 1:9-12; 4:12-13
    I Timothy 2:1; 4:5
    James 5:14-18

24. *Martyrdom.* The ability to stand firm on divinely inspired convictions and divinely directed ministries without equivocation or ulterior motives.

    Acts 6:10, 15; 7:54-60
    I Corinthians 13:3

    I Thessalonians 2:2
    I Timothy 6:12

25. *Service.* The ability to elevate any deed or service that aids the church or another person to a form of worship without concern or desire for rank, popularity, position, or recognition.

    Matthew 4:11
    Mark 1:31
    Luke 10:40
    John 12:2

    Acts 6:1
    Romans 12:7
    Galatians 6:2, 10
    Titus 3:4

26. *Spirit-Music.* The ability to create or perform lyrics and musical tunes as messages from God to inspire others to Christian service, to win others to Christ, or to tell the story of God's love and grace.

    II Chronicles 5:11-14
    Psalm 57:7-9

    I Corinthians 14:15
    Ephesians 5:19

27. *Craftmanship.* The ability to use physical materials and artistic skills to create, mold, carve, sculpt, draw, design, paint, repair,

or photograph items necessary for spiritual nurture, faith development, and caring ministries.

Exodus 35:20-35; 36:1-3

28. *Exorcism.* The ability to use faith, prayers, spirit-music, or other spiritual gifts to liberate the persons from debilitating and hindering forces and evil circumstances to free them to use their gifts effectively to serve the body of Christ and others through the church.

I Samuel 16:14-23
Matthew 8:16-17; 12:43-45
Mark 1:24; 16:17
Luke 9:1, 49-50; 10:17; 11:25

Acts 5:16; 8:6-8; 16:16; 19:11-12
I Corinthians 2:6-8; 10:20-21
Ephesians 6:10-18
Colossians 1:13-15; 2:20

29. *Battle.* The ability to use spiritual, physical, or psychological energies with righteous force enough to confront and overcome evil that hinders the church's mission to do God's will.

Deuteronomy 31:6
Joshua 1:6-9
II Samuel 10:12
Daniel 10:19
Acts 23:11

I Corinthians 16:13
Ephesians 6:10-17
I Thessalonians 2:2
I Timothy 6:12

30. *Humor.* The ability to bring laughter and joy to situations and relationships to relieve tension, anxiety, or conflict and to heal and free emotions and energies needed for effective ministries.

John 13:6-15
I Corinthians 12:12-24

Galatians 5:12

31. *Miracles*. The ability to do powerful works that transcend our perception of natural laws and means to free the church or individuals from conditions that restrict needed ministries.

Genesis 18:14
Mark 9:38-40; 16:17-18
Luke 1:37
Acts 4:30; 5:1-10, 12; 13:11
I Corinthians 2:4; 12:10, 28

32. *Voluntary Poverty*. The ability to live a simple, conservative, and unencumbered life free of material responsibilities to devote large amounts of time, energy, and skills to essential ministries.

Mark 1:18, 20; 10:21
Acts 2:45; 4:34-35
I Corinthians 13:3
II Corinthians 8:9

Personal Reflection

- Identify which of the spiritual gifts you believe you have.

- Are there any gifts listed that are of no consequence to the church today?

- What gifts do you most desire?

- After you have completed the Grace-Gifts Discovery Inventory in the Appendix, compare your results to your response to the first question. What about the third question? Are you actively exercising or operating in these gifts?

Discuss with your Pastor

- The various manifestations of the Spirit you believe are actively working in the church you attend.

- The results of your Grace-Gifts Discovery Inventory.

APPENDIX A

GRACE-GIFTS DISCOVERY INVENTORY
Taken from Rediscovering Our Spiritual Gifts *by Charles V. Bryant*

Prior to taking this inventory, consider the following imperatives:
  (1) Pray sincerely for God's guidance. God wants you to know and utilize your gifts.
  (2) Do not relate these to your profession or occupation.
  (3) Do not consider how you relate to your family or what you do for your family.
  (4) Make every effort to rank all items in relationship to what you have done and experienced within the church.

Rank each of the following statements according to how it describes your experience or strong inclination – not how to make you look good: Much=3, Some=2, Little=1, or None=0. Write the number of the value in the blank to the right of the statement.

1. I have a special sense of right and wrong, justice and injustice, and need to express it to others. _____
2. I enjoy working with and spiritually caring for groups of persons. _____
3. It is easy for me to aid persons in learning relevant information about the Bible and Christian living. _____
4. What I understand as divine truth is easy for me to apply to daily living. _____
5. Discovering or recognizing spiritual meanings and divine principles comes easily for me. _____
6. I delight in working with and encouraging depressed or apathetic persons. _____
7. I intuitively spot what is real or phony in other people and situations. _____

Grace-Gifts Discovery Inventory

8. It is easy and enjoyable to manage my income so that I may give liberally to God's work. _____
9. The needs of others, more than my own or my family's excite me to Christian action. _____
10. Persons with problems and pain attract my attention more quickly than others without apparent needs. _____
11. Other cultures, races, and languages offer no hurdles for my Christian service. _____
12. I bring persons to Christ through my personal efforts. _____
13. I offer friendship and other services to strangers without hesitation and fear. _____
14. I know God actively and purposely works in every event and circumstance. _____
15. I enjoy showing others how they can work for God in the church and the community. _____
16. I am energized by and feel joy when organizing a project, working out details, and getting others in the right places to reach a goal. _____
17. I feel that suffering is one of God's ways of accomplishing a divine purpose in life. _____
18. My prayers are a source of healing for others. _____
19. I pray in words or thoughts that I don't understand. _____
20. I understand and can interpret what others say or pray in words or phrases they do not know as a language. _____
21. Leaving the comforts of home, friends, and my church to serve other Christians elsewhere appeals to me. _____
22. Do I ever wonder how spiritually rewarding it must be not to be married? _____
23. I have a special sense of knowing when others need my prayers. _____
24. I am willing and able to endure any hardship to demonstrate God's love and power to others. _____
25. I enjoy doing most anything for the church and others if it serves Christ's purposes. _____
26. I sing praises to God with tunes I've never heard or learned. _____

27. I have a special sense about whether church buildings honor God and aid Christian discipleship. _____
28. When someone is an obvious victim of an alien evil desire, I feel a strong need to pray for that person's deliverance in the name of Jesus. _____
29. I enjoy debating persons who discredit the value of the church or Christian faith and usually win their esteem. _____
30. I enjoy making others laugh. _____
31. I become aware of surprisingly powerful results from some things I do for God's work. _____
32. A fulfilling life, to me, should be simple and free from obligations that do not directly support kingdom living. _____
33. Definite information and insights about personal and social evils come to me for correcting and guiding the church. _____
34. I enjoy being with and serving the same people over long periods of time. _____
35. I find it easy and enjoyable to explain what the New Testament teaches about Christian living. _____
36. What appears to be a complicated problem for others, I intuitively understand and solve. _____
37. I have special insights to God's will for the church and righteous living that do not always come from studying the Bible or having a formal education. _____
38. I inspire and motivate others to do things for their spiritual well-being. _____
39. Something inside stirs me to question whether some things are from God, human nature, or evil. _____
40. Giving my time, talents, energy, and money is a cheerful experience of Christian living. _____
41. The main reason I do things for others is to help them in their spiritual growth. _____
42. I have immediate compassion for persons who have spiritual, emotional, or physical pain. _____
43. Ministering to persons who are different from me would be an exciting ministry. _____

Grace-Gifts Discovery Inventory

44. I get great joy from telling persons who have not professed Christ as Savior how he became my Savior and how he wants to become theirs. _____
45. I sense a special opportunity for ministry when my normal routine is interrupted by guests or strangers. _____
46. I have a blessed assurance that God is involved in everything, small or great, and is working out a divine plan. _____
47. I seem to be "out front" of others in faith ventures, and many follow my example. _____
48. Organizing ideas, people, resources, and schedules is easy and enjoyable for me. _____
49. I identify my pains and tragedies as sharing the suffering of our Lord. _____
50. Because of my specific prayers, certain unhealthy conditions change for the good. _____
51. I experience a spiritual presence and power when I pray or chant in a wordless form. _____
52. When others deliver inspired messages in words and sounds not known by the hearers, I am able to explain. _____
53. I yearn to go to new places to proclaim Christ and to help establish another group of believers. _____
54. I can be a whole person outside a social or legal bond with one person. _____
55. When I hear requests for prayers, I eagerly and immediately begin to pray. _____
56. The prospect of loss or gain because of my faith in Jesus Christ causes me no abiding concern. _____
57. I do most anything that needs to be done because everything is an opportunity to glorify God. _____
58. I easily discern when music is a performance rather than a spiritual aid to worship. _____
59. I recognize that religious symbols are essential for enhancing Christian fellowship and worship. _____
60. I know when there are conflicts between evil and good forces, and I feel that God wants to use me to eradicate the evil. _____

A Charge to Preach

61. I have such strong feelings about the rightness of the church's role in the affairs of life that I stand read to defend it at whatever cost. _____
62. It is easy for me to spot humor in most situations, even serious and painful ones. _____
63. I feel mysteriously connected to a divine power when doing ministries of Christ for others. _____
64. I enjoy having a minimal income and no debts so that my interests and energies may be put to Christ's use. _____
65. I am stirred by the modern relevance of biblical teachings and principles and must speak my mind about them. _____
66. I find it easy and enjoyable to sustain deep relationships with a variety of people. _____
67. I devote much time to biblical and spiritual studies to share with others. _____
68. When I am faced with several options, my choices result in positive effects. _____
69. I understand and can connect different Bible stories and teachings without difficulty. _____
70. I consider it important that others gain strength and comfort from my ministries. _____
71. I am deeply disturbed when something seems wrong and exuberant over what seems right without any apparent reason for my judgment; eventually, my feelings prove correct. _____
72. When there is a call for donations, I feel excited enough to do all I can. _____
73. Doing routine tasks is not dull or drudgery for me if it helps others in their spiritual journey. _____
74. Doing something for persons in nursing homes, hospitals, hospices, and other caregiving places satisfies me greatly. _____
75. I have something of value to contribute to people in socio-economic, racial, or language situations radically different from mine. _____
76. I have deeper feelings for people who need to know Christ as Savior than for regular church members who already know Christ. _____

Grace-Gifts Discovery Inventory

77. I make strangers and newcomers comfortable in my presence. _____

78. To me, God's will is more important than either a deliverance from the unpleasant or an acquisition of the wonderful. _____

79. I have dreams and visions of new ministries that the church can offer, and I enjoy helping to set long-range goals for the church's ministries. _____

80. When I take on projects, my planning, detailing, and supervising result in people friendliness and smooth operation. _____

81. I see God's powerful love in my sorrow, hardships, pain, or loss. _____

82. God heals the physically, mentally, socially, financially, or spiritually sick through my efforts. _____

83. I feel spiritually right and normal to pray or to give praise to God with utterances unlike any language I know. _____

84. I delight in understanding and translating for others who speak with unintelligible words. _____

85. People accept what I say about spiritual matters without offering rebuttals. _____

86. The divine purpose of singleness is freedom to give more time to ministries for our Lord and his church. _____

87. Praying is my most enjoyable spiritual activity. _____

88. I am stubborn and unyielding in my insistence on what Christ means to me and to everyone. _____

89. I think of cleaning, clerical work, caring for buildings, ushering, babysitting, mowing, setting up chairs, and other acts as significant ways to worship God. _____

90. My music becomes a God-given means for preparing souls for a special anointing of grace. _____

91. I feel a special closeness to God when I build, make, or repair something related to the church and God's people. _____

92. At times I feel that my praying is a battlefield on which evil and good forces are battling for control over someone or some event. _____

93. I feel like a Christian soldier at war with evil, not people. _____

A Charge to Preach

94. I experience fun and entertainment as vital parts of the practice of Christian faith. _____
95. Though I do not intend it, extraordinary things occur when I assert special efforts for Christ and his church. _____
96. God does not want me to have worldly possessions, so that the kingdom may claim my time and strength. _____
97. I experience urges to speak God's message that prove to be timely and needed by others. _____
98. I find it easy to carry many concerns for many persons with a variety of needs. _____
99. I enjoy arduous and long hours of study to make God's word plain and easy to understand for others. _____
100. The themes of love, righteousness, holiness, peace, and discipleship are easy for me to translate into practical acts of daily Christian living. _____
101. Meanings and overtones of biblical themes are more important than mere facts, names, or dates. _____
102. I urge others to believe their sufferings and trials will develop their patience, strength, and hope. _____
103. I easily detect spiritual truth and error when others see no cause to question the difference. _____
104. I do not care how the church uses my contributions, since what I give is unto God. _____
105. I am satisfied just to serve others, even if I never get recognized for what I do. _____
106. I feel the discomforts and pains of others, and I get relief only by doing something to relieve theirs. _____
107. I daydream about living and serving God among people of other nations, races, and cultures. _____
108. I believe that the primary purpose of the church is to win persons to Christ. _____
109. I really love meeting new people and learning about them, and I am eager to greet them to make them feel welcome. _____

Grace-Gifts Discovery Inventory

110. I know God is real; though circumstances appear hard, cruel, and impossible to others, I relax in knowing that God is in control. _____
111. Others say that my influence has guided them to gain new directions and achievements in life. _____
112. All ministries should be amply planned, sufficiently staffed, and carried out to the fullest detail. _____
113. God uses my sorrows to bring about radical changes for the good of other persons and events. _____
114. Through my counseling, touch, or prayer, illnesses disappear. _____
115. In my private devotions, I pray both with words I understand and with utterances I don't understand. _____
116. I interpret messages from spiritual languages to build up the members of the church. _____
117. I enjoy spending lots of time visiting other churches to aid them in their services to Christ. _____
118. God gives special relief from sexual needs and frustrations to single persons. _____
119. I am moved to pray for others, even though I may not know them, and for conditions about which I know very little or nothing at the time. _____
120. I prefer dying painfully for Jesus Christ than dying painlessly without knowing him personally. _____
121. Because of a special closeness I feel to God when I do any kind of work for the church, I am quick to volunteer. _____
122. When I sing or play music, I feel spiritual energy flowing through me. _____
123. I am spiritually fulfilled when engaged in creative and artistic physical or manual work for the good of the church. _____
124. I need to know and to name the demonic force to pray or work effectively for its elimination. _____
125. I view the church as an army of the Lord and myself as a part of its special victory force. _____

A Charge to Preach

126. I recognize amusing events and statements in the Bible that most people do not see. _____
127. I experience unexpected and unsolicited inner promptings to do some service for Christ and the church and learn later of unbelievable results. _____
128. I feel it is important for me to identify with the poor to build their confidence in my service to them. _____
129. I receive special insights for warnings, cautions, instructions, and encouragements to give to the church for its effectiveness and preservation. _____
130. I have special feelings for Christians who have strayed and for church members who are inactive. _____
131. It gives me pleasure to explain God's word in such a way that others learn how to live righteously. _____
132. I see God's will clearly and how to apply it to personal living and church ministries. _____
133. It is clear to me how biblical teachings relate to universal and timeless needs of human life. _____
134. Through my personal involvement, troubled, depressed, or confused persons receive strength and composure in the Lord. _____

135. I have a special sensing for false teachings, erroneous judgments, and insincere and dishonest behavior. _____
136. My giving as a Christian is determined not by my special interests, ability, or resources but by joy and gratitude. _____
137. People are so important to me that everything I do as a Christian must be done for their good. _____
138. I have strong inclinations toward people with troubles and special needs, and I get joy from helping them. _____
139. My heart goes out to the unchurched, underprivileged, and others the church is not touching with its gospel of Christ. _____

140. While talking with anyone who appears not to be a Christian, I experience a strong desire to win him or her to Christ. _____

Grace-Gifts Discovery Inventory

141. I do not mind and am not afraid to welcome unknown persons into my home. _____
142. Even when wrong prevails and situations threaten with hopelessness, I sense that God's blessing is forthcoming. _____
143. People seek me out to lead them in their faith ventures. _____
144. Carrying the responsibility for organizing group activities toward stated goals is something I enjoy and do well. _____
145. My witness in affliction and trouble has been used by God to lead others to experience the joy of Christ in their hardships. _____
146. Directly through my various efforts, healings occurred that did not come from natural or medical means. _____
147. Praying or praising God in wordless sounds and phrases gives me a sense of unhindered and intimate communication with God. _____
148. I receive direct clarifications of divine messages for the good of the church through persons who, to others, speak in unintelligible gibberish. _____
149. When I visit from church to church and have occasion to speak, I feel a sense of authority in spiritual matters that comes only from God. _____
150. Being single and enjoying it never discounts the value of marriage for others but frees me to serve the church more fully. _____
151. I feel urges to pray for others to be empowered for effective ministries. _____
152. Whatever the costs, I do not hesitate to tell others about God's love in Jesus Christ. _____
153. It does not matter how menial or mundane my task; my joy is doing it for Christ. _____
154. I can tell whether certain hymns and types of music are spiritually suitable for the occasion. _____
155. Engaging my manual skills for Christ and his church is a special form of prayer and ministry for me. _____

A Charge to Preach

156. God uses my obedience to free others of evil forces. _____
157. I think of unbelievers not as enemies but as persons in need of a strong Christian influence and commander. _____
158. I use wholesome jokes and laughable statements to relieve others of pressure, anxiety, or suffering. _____
159. I feel mystically empowered by the presence of God when doing some things that others may consider insignificant, strange, or impossible. _____
160. Having little of this world's goods doesn't make me feel inferior to others or left out of God's grace. _____

The numbers in the chart refer to the numbered inventory items you just ranked. Look back at the inventory to see the value you assigned each question, and pencil in that value (3, 2, 1, or 0) next to the number of that question in each box. After listing the 160 values, add your total horizontally for each row in the chart (excluding the printed numbers). Put the sum on the line in the Total column. The sum ranges from 0 to 15.

The total for each row indicates the extent to which you may be gifted or inclined to operate the gift named in the first column of the row. Look to see which gifts have the highest totals.

Grace-Gifts Discovery Inventory

Gifts	Values					Total
Prophecy	1	33	65	97	129	
Pastor	2	34	66	98	130	
Teaching	3	35	67	99	131	
Wisdom	4	36	68	100	132	
Knowledge	5	37	69	101	133	
Exhortation	6	38	70	102	134	
Discernment	7	39	71	103	135	
Giving	8	40	72	104	136	
Helps	9	41	73	105	137	
Mercy	10	42	74	106	138	
Missionary	11	43	75	107	139	
Evangelism	12	44	76	108	140	
Hospitality	13	45	77	109	141	
Faith	14	46	78	110	142	
Leadership	15	47	79	111	143	
Administration	16	48	80	112	144	
Suffering	17	49	81	113	145	
Healings	18	50	82	114	146	
Prayer Language	19	51	83	115	147	
Interpretation	20	52	84	116	148	
Apostle	21	53	85	117	149	
Singleness	22	54	86	118	150	
Intercessory Prayer	23	55	87	119	151	
Martyrdom	24	56	88	120	152	
Service	25	57	89	121	153	
Spirit-Music	26	58	90	122	154	
Craftsmanship	27	59	91	123	155	
Exorcism	28	60	92	124	156	
Battle	29	61	93	125	157	
Humor	30	62	94	126	158	
Miracles	31	63	95	127	159	
Poverty	32	64	96	128	160	

A Preacher's Prayer

Who has believed our report O Lord
And to whom has your mighty hand been revealed
Buried deep within the treasures of your word
I stand boldly before the tree on which you were killed

A charge to preach entrusted me
By thou my God to glorify
Yea though I dwell among a sinful nation
For you I live and for you I must die

As a prisoner of the Lord Jesus
And an Ambassador for the King of kings
I preach to a lost and blinded people
Who are bought with diamond rings

I pray thee Lord for a Shepherd's word
That I may hide it deep within my heart
To let my light shine so before men
That they will have need not to depart

Order my steps this and every day
That I may not sin against thee
Send down thine anointing
And I pray that you would lead me

Let the words of my mouth
Be acceptable in thy sight
Regulate the meditation of my heart
That I may preach with all my might.

- Amen

A CHARGE TO PREACH: *Letters to a Young Preacher*

Selected Bibliography

Blanchard, Ken and Hodges, Phil *Lead Like Jesus* Nashville: Thomas Nelson Publishers, 2005.

Blanchard, Ken and Hodges, Phil *The Servant Leader* Nashville: J Countryman, 2003.

Bryant, Charles V *Rediscovering Our Spiritual Gifts* Nashville: Upper Room Books, 1991.

Carter, Mack King *A Catechism for Baptist* Florida: Four G Publishers, Inc., 1997.

Cordeiro, Wayne *Attitudes That Attract Success* Ventura: Regal Books, 2001.

Flippin, Sr., William E *God's Order* Highland Park: Mall Publishing Co., 2007.

Kennedy, D. James and Newcombe, Jerry *What if the Bible Had Never Been Written?* Colorado Springs: Nelson Books, 1998.

Lewis, Ralph L. and Lewis, Gregg *Learning to Preach Like Jesus* Westchester: Crossway Books, 1989.

Odom, Jeremy W *Preaching that Empowers God's People* Natchitoches: Big O Publishing Group, 2016.

Ortberg, John *Soul Keeping* Grand Rapids: Zondervan, 2014.

Peterson, Eugene *Living the Message* San Francisco: HarperCollins Publishers, 1996.

Richards, Larry *Spiritual Warfare, Jesus' Way* Minneapolis: Baker Publishing Group, 2014

Selected Bibliography

Scott, Jr., Manuel *The Quotable Manuel Scott, Sr.* Morris Publishing, 2014.

Spurgeon, Charles H *Lectures to My Students* Grand Rapids: Baker Book House, 1977.

Stokes, Jeaninne *Baileyisms* Arlington: JStokes Publishing, 2015.

Stott, John R. W. *Your Mind Matters* Illinois: InterVarsity Press, 1972.

Vines, Jerry and Shaddix, Jim *Power in the Pulpit* Chicago: Moody Publishers, 1999.

www.ingramcontent.com/pod-product-compliance
Lightning Source LLC
Chambersburg PA
CBHW050440010526
44118CB00013B/1612